THE CONSCIENCE OF THE UNIVERSITY *and Other Essays*

To Dr. and Mrs. John Irwin

Hazel H. Ransom

July 20, 1983

Harry Huntt Ransom

Edited by Hazel H. Ransom

The Conscience of the University

of the University

and Other Essays

UNIVERSITY OF TEXAS PRESS
AUSTIN

First edition, 1982

Requests for permission to reproduce material from this work
should be sent to Permissions, University of Texas Press, Box
7819, Austin, Texas 78712.

Library of Congress Cataloging in Publication Data:

Ransom, Harry Huntt, 1908–
    The conscience of the university, and other essays.
    1. Education, Higher—Addresses, essays, lectures.
2. Intellectual life—Addresses, essays, lectures.
3. Ransom, Harry Huntt, 1908–   .   4. Educators—
United States—Biography.   I. Ransom, Hazel H.
II. Title.
LB2325.R28   378   82–4890
ISBN 0–292–71078–X   AACR2
ISBN 0–292–71080–1 (special)

Contents

Harry Ransom

Harry Huntt Ransom

November 22, 1908 – April 19, 1976

$\mathbf{B}$ORN in Galveston, Texas, Harry Ransom spent almost all of his professional career at The University of Texas at Austin. He earned degrees from the University of the South at Sewanee (B.A., Phi Beta Kappa, 1928) and Yale University (M.A., 1930; Ph.D., 1938). He studied at Harvard University (1929–30) and in England at the University of London (1939). He received a Doctor of Literature degree from the University of the South and other honorary degrees from the University of North Dakota, University of Dallas, Baylor University, Trinity University, Texas Christian University, Stephen F. Austin State University, Southern Methodist University, and Colorado School of Mines.

Joining The University of Texas in 1935 as instructor in English, he advanced through the academic ranks: assistant professor, 1938; associate professor, 1946; professor, 1947. From 1942 to 1946 he served as an officer in the U.S. Army Air Force and in 1947 was awarded the Legion of Merit for his work in editorial intelligence.

His administrative career began in 1951 when he became assistant dean of the Graduate School. In 1953 he was appointed associate dean of the Graduate School; in 1954, dean of the College of Arts and Sciences; in 1957, vice-president and provost; in 1960, president; in 1961, chancellor of The University of Texas System. After his retirement from the chancellorship in 1971, as chancellor emeritus he continued his work in the development of special research collections and prepared materials for a history of The University of Texas, a project that was incomplete at the time of his death.

His broader interests were evidenced by his work with literary periodicals. From 1938 to 1941 he was coeditor (with J. Frank Dobie and Mody C. Boatright) of the Texas Folklore Publications (volumes XIV–XVII). From 1952 to 1957 he was associate editor of the *Southwestern Historical Quarterly*. In 1958 he founded the *Texas Quarterly*, which achieved international recognition; he served as chairman of the editorial board until his death in 1976.

His principal research interests were in the fields of copyright law, bibliography, Texas history, and eighteenth- and nineteenth-century literary history. In 1939 he organized the research program for the International Copyright League in London and was chairman of the league's historical commission for several years. Among his publications were *Bibliography of English Copyright History* (1948), *Notes of a Texas Book Collector, 1850–1899* (1950), *The First Copyright Statute* (1956), *English Copyright Cases, 1660–1775*, of which he was associate editor (1956), and scores of articles, addresses, and editorials, exemplified by the texts in the following pages.

Throughout his teaching and administrative years, one of his principal concerns was the individual student. He originated or fostered many programs to improve the quality of teaching and research and was active in attracting private support to advance this goal. Among these programs were the twenty-four–hour student counseling service, the Provisional Admissions Program for highly motivated students who were unable to meet the entrance requirements, student scholarships, such honors programs as Plan II for the Bachelor of Arts degree and the Junior Fellows, the Program in Criticism lecture series that brought distinguished literary visitors to the campus, and the overall concept and construction of the Undergraduate Library and Academic Center, with its open-shelf library and audiovisual facilities. To commemorate Ransom's own brilliance as a teacher, one of his former students inaugurated a Harry Ransom award for excellence in teaching, to be given annually to a faculty member in the College of Liberal Arts.

He was elected or appointed to numerous educational, bibliophilic, and research organizations, including the Carnegie Foundation for the Advancement of Teaching, the Grolier Club, and national commissions on libraries, White House fellows, patents, the health professions, and the Supreme Court history.

Most observers believe that his most lasting contribution is the Humanities Research Center with its vast collections, housed largely in the building that in 1974 was named the Harry Ransom Center. Because of the HRC collections, which include literature, the history of science, iconography, theater arts, photography, and cartography, the U.T. Austin library was cited in 1970 by Anthony Hobson in his book *Great Libraries* as one of the thirty-two leading libraries in Western Europe and North America. It was one of only five great libraries in the United States listed by Hobson. One of the principal adornments of the center, incidentally, is the Pforzheimer copy of the Gutenberg Bible, dedicated to Ransom's memory and donated in large part by the Chancellor's Council, of which Ransom was founder.

In summing up Harry Ransom's role in U.T. library development, his colleague, former Chancellor Logan Wilson, concludes: "What once was a good library is now one of the best. This is a splendid memorial for a man who has said, 'Books have always been my principal occupation and one of my most profound personal pleasures.' "

Preface

SINCE Harry Ransom's death in 1976, I have examined most of his papers, including both literary texts and official documents. From the mass of his essays and addresses on the cultural resources of The University of Texas and the Southwest, I have selected eighteen that represent various facets of his concerns: the educational and social role of the university, the potential of Texas in that cultural and educational context, the student and the teacher as principals in the academic community, specific academic disciplines (here represented by only three), and, finally, the world of books and libraries, his most profound academic interest since it encompassed for him the broadest basis of learning, embracing the collection of knowledge from the humanities through the sciences.

Available elsewhere are essays that comment on such further concerns as administrative policy and the role of alumni in university planning and support, analytical essays on specific campus problems, and comments on student and faculty programs that are directly identified with his years.

In editing the materials included, I have made textual omissions for the sake of conciseness and have undertaken other minor revisions, always respecting the author's essential meaning. Wherever the author has referred to incidents or facts with deliberate omission of names or dates, I have preserved the spirit of his intent and made no attempt to supply specifics. In only one essay, "The Collector and Copyright," have I attempted to update the author's statements—this because of recent changes in copyright law.

I am indebted to a number of Harry's colleagues who have read the material at various points of its progress toward the present form. I owe special gratitude to Dr. Thomas M. Cranfill, the earliest reader, whose sensitive insight was invaluable; to Dr. Miguel González-Gerth for his skillful eye to text and concept; to Dr. William Rea Keast for his keen literary and editorial overview; to Dr. Logan Wilson for his professionally expert judgment of the project; to Professor James M. Treece, who advised on points of recent law concerning copyright; and to Esther R. Moore for organization of the Ransom papers for the Archives.

I am specially grateful to Mr. and Mrs. O. Scott Petty for their unflagging interest in the project and their material support of the book. I know that Harry would be pleased that this volume is being published during a University of Texas centennial year.

Hazel H. Ransom
1981

THE CONSCIENCE OF THE UNIVERSITY *and Other Essays*

The Conscience of the University

Address, Commencement, University of Dallas, 1971

As TO the definition of a word I will keep repeat-
ing, I do not take *conscience* to be a psychiatrical term for sparking
gaps between the university's id and ego, or its ego and super-
ego. Nor is my title borrowed from comparative theology or
church affiliations of early American universities. For these comments, the popular definition "a still small voice" is sufficient.
In that old folk sense there is an essential in every university
process that can be called "conscience." Because academic conscience does not rely upon either inherited piety or new jargon
about recurring crises, the longer university perspective is
relevant.

Here is a somewhat discouraging quotation from the receding
past: "American higher education as we have known it will
never be the same again. We have watched total disillusionment
with the belief that a war or wars can be the salvation of democracy. We have seen the failure of applied scientific knowledge to
solve the problems of both government and society. We have
gone through a decade of false optimism and foolish extravagance
only to face inevitable dismay among elders and disillusionment
in youth. We have piled up facts without proceeding toward
wisdom. The university's mission must change or it must be
abandoned."

Written in 1930, these sentences were addressed mainly to
problems confronted by the administration of Herbert Hoover,
one of the country's great engineers who was also one of the

world's greatest humanitarians. The pessimism was prologue to depression, protest marches, and breadlines. It was also a prediction of university experiments called variously "progressive," "general," "remedial," and "adult." I suggest that in any year we read and listen to such generalizations with healthy detachment.

In the period of an earlier "silent generation" many administrators were beseeching the press to pay more attention to educational problems. Two decades later, when attention became severe and almost continuous scrutiny, the educational world blamed "instant media" in print, picture, and sound for exaggerating disruption.

In similar, natural change, those who decried youth's search for financial security from 1930 to 1960 now decry youth's doubts about ultimate satisfaction in material goods. Young people, who have never been inclined in any Western republic to forego scoffing at their elders, now make youthful discoveries of the ancient fact of human fallibility. Only the terms differ: leaders who once were said to have feet of clay are lately charged with having rocks in the head.

One exercise that conscience imposes upon intelligence is to get words straight. Never before has educational vocabulary been so quickly exhausted or so deviously twisted. Words like *excellence, revolution, freedom, responsibility, goodness, power,* and *governance* are less useful because so often they have been misused and abused.

Because of arbitrary detachment and preoccupation with academic crisis, the still small voice of the university is not always heard. It cannot be made audible solely by charters, catalogues, tables of organization, resolutions, or commencement speeches. It can be drowned out completely by name-calling, protest, bull-horn rhetoric, and blame-shifting. It can be buried in fat educational silence, which clings to everything that is self-serving and rejects the recognition of our quite natural but indefensible selfishness. It is diminished by loose argument just as it is diminished by prim, hypocritical avoidance of plain uncomfortable facts about education.

Yet this conscience of the university has much to say. It says that patient understanding rather than violence leads to workable solutions between two persons or among two hundred million. It reminds us that during centuries of struggle on our somewhat flattened globe there have been turnabouts in the affairs of men brought on by rational process more often than by open conflict. It reminds us that custom, belief, and tradition have been reformed or brought into being more often by awareness of the common good and by common consent than by hot or lukewarm or frigid prejudice.

Tons of printed paper and miles of tape have left us numb to the meaning of major events in the twentieth century. What would have been minor miracles of attainment in earlier periods have been written off as technological advancement. Often universities have seemed to be waking from a nightmare of progress. Too often we have got a surfeit of answers before we had clarified the questions.

History can help us in our dismay. Giants of high conscience and resolved intellect—the Galileos, the Martin Luthers, the Saint Thomas Mores, the John Miltons, the Florence Nightingales—are not wraiths of the past. The university's conscience reminds us that people who bore such names were accompanied by unnamed, mute, but very live contemporaries. True science and true saintliness had their best beginnings in joint concern for knowledge and mankind, concern for both wisdom and the woe of others.

The search for wisdom, sprung from the knowledge of the needy mind and the needy body, is still vivid in the university's conscience, though some may choose to flee from it into the clangor of today's fear and hatred. There are no academic earmuffs for that noise, no patent medicine for those needs. There is no system of privilege in justice, equity, or opportunity. In human suffering there is no generation gap. At the hour of death there are no rigged confrontations, no unnegotiable demands for man to make, no amnesty.

What has all this to do with the university's conscience?

Everything. Everything, because all that a university is now or can become relates to a simple concept, man's fate. To that primary issue we must keep returning, however we are detained by degree programs, faculty organization, administration, admissions tests and signed diplomas, championships and centers for research, relevant and irrelevant experiment, dedication to causes and transient experience.

The responsible university has made its greatest contribution by sticking to its own principles. Its greatest undertaking has not been a convenient association of prescribed rule and random activity. It has been the profession of inseparable freedoms and responsibilities.

In good conscience, such a university opens paths for each of its members to pursue knowledge according to his or her need. That is an old precept and still a sound one, but it has never been sufficient for complete education. Moving outward, self-knowledge gropes toward an understanding of others. A paraphrase of Francis Bacon would translate "others" to mean "all others."

In trying to understand all mankind, we cannot proceed from tallies of the billions of diversities shown forth by human beings, past and present, living and dead. In lonely fact, none of us can ever know more than a tiny fraction of humanity. Hence our only hope of true understanding proceeds from unchanging belief in the unity of life—its conditions, aspirations, and final destiny—as well as willing recognition of individual differences.

Within this context, the alumni of a university become special guardians of the university's conscience. Alumni go out as permanent members of their university's community. In the sense of St. Augustine, it is their initial task to glean the good of harvests that they did not sow. The good is there, as surely as the seasons have turned. It is their main task to help sow a new harvest of good for a future that wise men do not dare predict.

The Steel Glass of Education

Address, Honors Day, Lamar University, Beaumont, 1965

PART of the title, some of you will recognize, is borrowed from a much underrated writer named Gascoigne. The "steel glass," to oversimplify, is simply the mirror that reflects truly and that is capable of reflecting differences. Education needs such a steel glass today. No institutionalized aspect of modern life is so prolific of self-examination and self-criticism as the campus. If you have attended many sessions of student committees (or faculty committee meetings), if you have read anything of the newspaper editorials, the monographs, the critiques, the proceedings, and the popular books, you know that "Johnny Can't Read," that teachers are underpaid, that nobody is really sure what general education is, that there will be more students in the year 2000 than this country can educate properly, that distant institutions seem better than ours (and that their excellence increases according to the miles distant), that we need to abolish the grade system (but we don't know what to substitute for it), that industry is raiding faculties (younger members of whom insist on having babies as well as books early), that academic freedom is a terrible problem, that eggheads don't like or aren't liked by any number of other groups in the commonwealth, that —well, this could go on a long time.

In brief, education is in a mess. One wonders, as he comes back from conventions or closes volumes that predict oncoming intellectual disaster, how this country, this state, or any institution has managed to stick together or stand up.

There must be something in the human being's mental climate that makes seed corn grow. There must be something to the loneliness of research, to the fine academic lesson of failure, to the ability of people to exchange ideas. Otherwise chaos would already be upon us.

I wish to make it clear that I do not object to any of these ancestral voices of doom and calamity, or the childish ones demanding more and more progressive education in the grades, or the loud and angry professional disagreements, or the academic prophets crying ruin across the country. Yet I wish to suggest that, in all this calamity howling, the good gets neglected for the sake of the bad. There are values that we can see if we hold the steel glass up to education. I think we should do it as a group. I think we should do it individually.

What one sees in that steel glass is so instantly apparent that no editorial, monograph, or speech about it is required. I don't think it is hard to recognize intellectual integrity, however hard it may be to cultivate.

I think that even my bifocaled generation can see in the steel glass the clear need of change, however hard it may be for us to welcome it in our classrooms, in our dissertations, in our term papers.

I am quite sure that younger people, perhaps still blinking from too much midnight oil burned at the altar of true-false examinations or a little dazzled by some discovery in a book or a laboratory, can see in this glass the future promise of clear and courageous thinking.

I realize that some, looking in this glass, will see a mathematical formula and others the musical words of old creeds. I do not think that the mathematical formula and the old creeds, if the steel glass is real steel and is really polished, will blur or contradict one another.

I have spoken figuratively. To mix the figures still further I must insist that the steel glass of education, representing the intellectual training provided by a college, is a very different optical arrangement from that glass which we are promised will some day be undarkened for us, though now we see through it darkly. I do not believe that human beings can escape the weariness of holding up this other hard, bright steel glass of intellectual training or avoid the terrible revelations that a realistic mirror of education must reveal.

Mirrors used to have inscriptions around the borders. As epigrams, they rank somewhere below the inscriptions on sundials.

> Fair the eyes and bright the hair
> Behold them here, O maiden fair!

> See thyself and turn away
> To live in beauty all this day.

> Alas, alas, the rounded glass
> Cannot reflect thee, perfect lass.

So far as I know, women are the target of all this tenth-rate rhyming. Nobody ever wrote mottoes for a man's shaving mirror.

If I were to write mottoes to be engraved upon the steel glass of education, they would have to be plain prose. One of them, even for moderns who think that our experiments have made us just about the smartest people who ever lived on this parlous earth, would have to read, "The answers are not all in." Another, aimed at people who believe that they have completed the job of education by amassing a certain number of college credits, would say, "One hundred twenty hours may make a college degree but do not make an education." Another would say, "He who cannot give away part of his education hasn't got one."

I think that the ideals have not gone out of education. Or what the professionals call "the objectives." Or the rewards (and I do not mean starting salaries; I mean the occasional sense of winning in one's private game against ignorance). What has largely gone out, for most people, is enjoyment. The steel glass, hard as it is, reflects a great deal of pure joy: Of the excitement of discovery. Of the wild surmise. Of the question put and answered, to no purpose whatever except that exchanging ideas is one of the distinctly human pleasures on this ball of rock, fire, mud, and flood water. Hard as it is, the steel glass mixes with the hideousness of things the quiet assurance of knowledge.

A man equipped with such a glass will never call himself educated, because he knows that the process never ends. He will never be concerned with the fact that he can sell his glass for $475 instead of $325—but he will know the reasons for the difference and will understand them. Looking in his glass, he will often be confused and have to squint. He will often be disturbed and have to compare other people's angles on the glass with his. He will often discover that he has seen wrong and that he will have to pay for his nearsightedness. He will be sometimes baffled and sometimes blinded. But one thing is certain. He will never be what entirely too many college students often are: uncertain of their values and bored.

Varieties of Ignorance

Address, Phi Beta Kappa, U.T. Austin, 1971

T H E academic world is filled with reminders about truth and wisdom, light and enlightenment. Witness the mottoes of numerous universities and organizations. I do not intend the title of these observations to imply that we should renounce the love of wisdom. The phrase "varieties of ignorance" reflects my own opinion that universities have paid too little attention to not-knowing.

One reason for this omission, of course, is that knowledge submits to measurement more easily than does the lack of it. It would be meaningless or totally misleading, for example, to convert an examination grade of 90 to an ignorance grade of minus 10.

The ratio of all that mankind has learned to all the gaps in knowledge—that is, to all that must be guessed or imagined—is vast. The vastness embarrasses even our guessing. It boggles our imagination. Undetermined truths and facts that still lie outside man's knowing are relevant to every student and scholar.

The calculation that more than three-fourths of the scientists and engineers born throughout millenniums on this pinched globe are still alive is widely advertised. Yet who is to say what percentage of discovery and understanding may open up to these living inquirers soon and to those who will succeed them after they are nonexistent? The understanding of the universe, the implications of death, the operation and operational limits of the human mind, such practical matters as ways of living together or making common sense of mere existence are not subjects on which, in the 1970s, humanity would score as high as 80. A great deal more than one-fifth of all possible wisdom lies waiting for the future.

As to particular varieties of ignorance, three contexts have fairly clear significance. The first concerns social interpretation; the second, highly personal attitudes toward not-knowing; and the third, ignorance as a practical concern of universities.

For centuries ignorance has been at least occasional subject for reflection. Some persons—real persons and fictional characters—have been downcast about the human lot to the point of despair, as in the paraphrase of the Greek poet-dramatist:

> The happiest life is lived in ignorance
> Before man learns grief and rejoicing.

Others have been patly epigrammatic, and some epigrams have served to express vague ironies, such as the observation

> Where ignorance is bliss
> 'Tis folly to be wise.

The social, philosophical, and rhetorical zeal with which the qualities of ignorance have been defined has often turned deceptive. When artists and writers have thought that they could detect a relationship between ignorance and blessed innocence, human beings called "noble savages" have sometimes been envied. Later scholars have pointed out that both the wisdom and the unhappiness of savages can escape idioms of civilization. You have to be one to judge one.

In earlier formal social contexts, systematic descriptions of ignorant existence by words like *nescience* endured only briefly. The impression that whole populations of humanity were destined by fate and by choice to continue in what Ruskin described as a kind of barnyard society has been disproved by social theory and outmoded by legislation and by vivid proof of intelligence among the untutored.

Today we sometimes face confusion when our society confronts new states of ignorance. The state of not-knowing may still result from natural condition or indolent choice. Today confusion rises dismayingly among surpluses of unmanageable knowledge: too many facts for universities to sort, too much information incoming at too fast a rate to be used while it is still more or less reliable. Hence our wistful hope invested in such devices as computers. Yet hope is not always matched by either man or his machines. When what the human cranium encases can't make the computer serve an instant purpose, some of us irrationally blame the machine and not our impractical expectations of it or our impatient inability to make it work.

As contrasted with social interpretation, subjective uses of ignorance vary enormously. Professed ignorance, sometimes real and sometimes feigned, can be merely defensive. Man pleads "I did not know" almost daily. Ignorance of common, constitutional, or statutory law, ignorance of the laws of "nature," ignorance of conditions and attitudes of a fellow man or a society of nations should be neither excuse nor confession of guilt but recognition of our limits and our need to enlarge those limits by both knowledge and understanding.

In personal terms, ignorance can also be a posture, a calculated act designed to produce a calculated effect. I once tried to draft speeches for a political candidate in another state. He refused to accept from his staff any text that was grammatical or that misled him into approximately correct pronunciation. In his role of ignorance he acted with great earnestness. Nor were his motives base. He would say sincerely, "I know less than the total of my constituency, but I care more about those men and women than they care about themselves." With that belief, he felt that the appearance of illiteracy gave him working ground. From that ground he ascended to high office, and his good works live after him.

Such benevolent, calculated ignorance is quite different, however, from flippant or resolved anti-intellectualism. Until magazines began to run cartoons about computers, they made periodic fun of subjects of academic research. This was during a period when it was comforting to report that only twelve men in the world knew what Einstein was talking or writing about. Such good-humored response to obscurities of knowledge does little harm. When response is moved by fear, which turns to hate, which can turn to persecution, the result is havoc. Witness the fortunes of scholars in Europe before World War II.

Anti-intellectualism should be countered at the start by forthright understanding and by equally forthright conviction. Expedient submission to book-burners and vilifiers of the search for freedom through truth is neither good strategy nor good tactics. It is, in long historic fact, treason against man's highest intellectual and spiritual potentials.

For centuries the universities carried on their combat with ignorance in what today would seem to be seclusion. Cloistered thought and intellectual battles for knowledge within university walls were not nearly so peaceful as some sentimental antiquarians would have us believe. Scholars alone or in company with their fellows had to confront not only querulousness and open quarrel but also clashes with ignorance in general, the hostilities of prejudgment, settled institutional prejudice, the hostility of the public. Some took great risks. Some early scholars, indeed, risked and lost their heads, and the loss was anatomical, not metaphorical.

Throughout these earlier centuries and in our generation, universities have had opportunity to use ignorance as well as knowledge. One use has been the encouragement of intellectual humility, a talent still much needed in every academic arena. Acknowledged ignorance can also be the start of rational discussion. Socrates made a personally disastrous but philosophically and pedagogically triumphant career of that intellectual position. He has had his modern imitators. Yet it is apparent that in the twentieth century there is still a shortage of free willingness to pursue ignorance impartially toward something like bare truth. Indeed, truth has sometimes seemed to pose a greater threat than hemlock to minds disposed to their own comfort.

Thus late, the university can make no special claims to comfort or self-satisfaction. To be self-satisfied in today's academic world is to be less than self-true. The ancient behest "Know thyself" applies not only to individual men and women but also to institutions. Hence the needs for self-criticism lie as heavy upon universities as upon other groups that acknowledge ignorance, profess belief, or undertake social uses of knowledge: the churches, for example, or the professions that act upon a body of learning and an expectation of changed experience and changeful discovery.

All this implies certain simple obligations of a university in a world manifestly conditioned by ignorance as well as knowledge:

— We are bound to acknowledge the reaches of the unknown whenever we boast the attainment of human intellect.

— Thus we are brought to humility by the same processes that allow us pride of knowledge. I mean vigorous and creative humility, not that empty, abject, and vain humbleness which is one of the seven deadly virtues.

— We are encouraged in tolerance of such true and honest ignorance as can become the threshold of honorable and truthful learning.

— We are reminded that, although knowledge is proper to mankind, it is not proprietary.

— Finally, we must learn to define ignorance before the fact and confess error after the fact.

So far as I know there is no list of rules about the life for which the love of wisdom can provide guidance to merely happy havens. For individuals and for universities we can only express hope for a voyage into new lessons, new learning, and renewed conscience, a hope worth cherishing both institutionally and personally.

Educational Resources in Texas

Texas Quarterly, Winter 1961*

I N an era of expanding plants and costly equipment, educational resources are often measured publicly by what is patently measurable: cubic footage, flat or rolling acres, and dollars for essential physical instruments of education. Among problems of education that raise immediate contradictions and ambiguities, this problem of physical resources is a basic one.

To emphasize physical assets may seem to minimize what is most important—the immaterial values, the assets of mental wealth, the resources of the mind. By comparison with spiritual values, physical equipment (like laboratories for scientific experiment, buildings to house libraries and art collections, machinery and space for the elaborate modern technics of instruction) is easy to discount. Every one of us has said that, given a choice between minds and mortar, we must choose minds; and we have meant every syllable of that choice. But today the historical Mark Hopkins and his hypothetical student would produce, from opposite ends of their log, nothing more than cultivated conversation, or perhaps an elementary course in forestry.

More than in any previous generation it is necessary to support the love of wisdom by the hard wares of education. We cannot deny to higher education its essential equipment: spectrometers, nuclear accelerators, electronic computers, bibliographical apparatus, and audiovisual aids. Deny these things, these mere things,

* Also published in *Texas, Today and Tomorrow*, edited by Herbert P. Gambrell (Dallas: Southern Methodist University Press, 1961).

and you lose well-trained and experienced minds to educational centers that provide them; at the same time you cheat native minds that stay at home, wistfully hoping that intelligence and ambition can somehow make up for empty laboratories and barren library shelves.

Physical resources come first, where they belong: they are the initial but not the final and formative resources for education in a state.

Of a state's educational resources, the chief is always personal —educated persons and a population that is constantly educable. Of such human resources, Texas has always had a notable, but not an inexhaustible, supply. More than one Ashbel Smith appeared between the swamps and the desert in nineteenth-century Texas. The fact that these men and women sowed the seeds of education on middle ground (which was mostly rock) and made those seeds grow is the most neglected fact in Texas history.

In planning for education, the founders of Texas were not unaware of the elder Greek city-state, the scholarly ways of medieval monks, and the magnificence that accompanied the magnanimity of certain Renaissance princes. Yet they talked, and talked, and talked straight, to their contemporaries—Hispanic, Scotch-Irish, Catholic, Protestant, Southern-plantation, and Tennessee-highland contemporaries, who joined the multiple-minded new American generation that first populated Texas. The gist of what they said was later carved in stone and then largely forgotten. We have revived some of it in fine resolutions for which we claim novelty and new educational ambitiousness. Ashbel Smith's estimates of intellectual resources in this state were modern enough. What is more important, they were durably true. Central to every estimate he made was the belief that the enlightened individual is both end and means of freedom in a state.

First we expect physical resources, next people capable of using them, and finally the program of education. Given minimum physical resources, a resourceful people will make its own program, about which the most important fact is that it changes. It must change. In early Texas undertakings of this kind, the dominant purpose was to conserve such education as would make a republic and later make a state, each in its turn sensitive to new cultural and economic conditions.

Within a six-month period in those first years, two apparently contradictory reports appeared in what passed for a newspaper in southern Texas. One was an account of the roundabout means by which volumes of a classical library were brought down river, around Gulf shores, and up bayou waterways to impermanent but hopeful communities in which the most active living things were horses and mosquitoes. The other was a bald announcement, put in an equivalent of today's banner headline, that Texas needed no more men of talent.

Both of these reports out of the early history of the state can be written off, the first as a frontier sentimentality about books, the second as anti-intellectualism on the frontier. Neither dismissal would be fair; neither would be historically accurate. The first was a calculated move against an environment that was still intellectually barren. The second was a spontaneous, if unrealistic, report that lawyers and doctors in Texas were obscuring if not outnumbering carpenters, mechanic workers, and tillers of an almost limitless but not very responsive soil. Both reports spoke to instant imperatives on the southwestern frontier. The works of the mind and the work of men's hands had made about equally futile impression, to that date, on a quarter-million square miles west of the country's main inland waterway. The first gesture was not futile: it led to the founding of Swante Palm's library in Austin. The second condition was not permanently repressive: several generations later, it had not discouraged cultivation of immeasurable acres and the probing of basement rock and upward sky.

There was, in those days, a poetry of opportunity in Texas. There were, besides, some inexorable facts, and the facts could not get along without the poetry. But poets in those days, who wrote constitutions and manifestoes and advertisements for immigration instead of rhymed verse, could not have made sense without hard-handed and harder-headed men who insisted on making necessity rhyme with hope for the Texas future. Today it might help educational planners to reread accounts of the agreement of those two frames of mind in early Texas.

Opportunity was here, abundant, before Oil City, long before Spindletop. It was a day when the most immediate problem in educational logistics was getting children to one-room schooling in flatbed wagons. It was a day when biblical lands were only colored pages in the back of family Bibles, an educational millennium before the advent of Israeli and Arabic engineering students to Texas universities. That millennium was compressed into something less than a century.

Texas must still write its educational prescriptions in such historical shorthand. That we are out of sorts with our educational calendar is a curious irony. Social demand and economic imperatives in Texas were updated after 1900. Between the bayous and the Permian Basin, wealth got made. But social esteem for ideas and for mentality capable of handling ideas slumped. Texas was wealthier in educational imagination between 1836 and 1916 than it has been since. In succeeding years we have often refused to acknowledge changes in time, in maps, in necessities, in obligations. The early Texans had almost nothing to support them but determination and perspective. We have kept our determination high; we have kept asserting it among ourselves to the point of anger and contention. Perspective? Perspective is what we need to recapture.

Hot contention, raucous argument, and loud protestation cannot kill a state's educational future. Only calm indifference, self-satisfied silence, and the deadly quiet negative will do education in. We can afford to make proper concessions among conflicting interests, formulary compromises among educational purposes, and fiscal adjustments in the good name of sound economy in the state. But one big fact should be kept straight: for popular ignorance, for a state's undereducation, there can be no price but public ignominy. The only cheap compromise with hard educational demands of the future will be industrial, social, and political defeat. In this business we know prices as well as values. Fancy talk and a talent for expediency are not going to change conditions that determine the educational fate of Texans. The future tragedy of this state, if it is to move toward a tragic conclusion, will be that men capable of wisdom were content to remain merely "smart."

It is part of wisdom to locate ourselves. Locale is an important frame for educational resources, which involve a sort of conceptual location as distinct from mere geography. The isles of Greece, the Rhine, New England are spirits of place as well as mere places. In similar ways, Texas has always been a distinct homesite of the mind. For those exiles who bolted (or tore themselves away) from easier eastern ways, Texas was the end of nowhere. As a frontier, as the great geographical pan of mountain and mesa and river and flat and brush and piney wood, Texas was at the farthest possible remove from centers of nineteenth-century American culture.

If you have not looked at big continental maps lately with the notion of plotting educational development and the location of educational resources, imagine such a map. Texas now lies central in it; central to two coasts, central among the Americas. It has moved from the end of nowhere into local and national and international focus.

Educational centrality is position; it also should be a state of activity. Confluence of ideas in motion makes steadier patterns upon a map than weather fronts or the lines describing mercantile routes. Movement of two-legged freight in and out of a region is no longer mere tourism. Not since the Middle Ages have great issues so often depended upon the meeting of minds that have traveled long distances. If Texas does not recognize its place in this wide concourse of the intellect and does not encourage this traffic in ideas, it will throw away its finest prospect for development. Although there are not many signs that we are drawing a Texas intellectual map upon this swinging compass, how else can we describe what will surely be the circles of future intellectual rotation? This conception of the educative world is not limited to academic speculation. It will inform the whole state's future sense of being. Ideas are at once a people's most perishable and most nearly permanent creation. As popular resources, they can be renewed. The people must renew them.

A constitution, a political platform, or an educational program can gain no new credence by running through the press one more time. It is durable only in the sense that it is credible, defensible only to the extent that a great majority of the people will defend it. Many economic and industrial concerns are quite properly limited and closed interests, but educational resources are not among them. They are everybody's business.

Society's wide concern for education is more complex than current criticisms of education lead us to believe. Education does not depend upon schooldom or upon mere knowing. Invention and creation, communication and interpretation, criticism and refinement are all part of the bringing-forth and the trying-out processes that society uses for the mind's products. Nor is the conservation of durable thinking, the holding fast of what has been proved good, diminished in importance by a new age that demands new modes and new minds.

In the newest social process nothing is more important than the identity and fast establishment of individual achievement among social valuations. A society really concerned with education will be concerned with scholar, scientist, writer, and artist as citizens and with their social meaning, what manner of citizens they are, and the social significance of what they do. The wealth created by such a citizenry is quite real, although it is wealth produced not so much by shrewd prospecting or canny investment as by allegiance to the right causes. Some of society's prosperity is maintained by asking the right questions and making the right guesses. These are not esoteric questions and private guesses. They are the cultural stock of the body politic.

In the history of Western civilization, chapters on immaterial wealth are stories of social ambiguity, economic irony, and outrageous contradiction. The history of Texas education is such a chapter.

Traditionally, education has been counted in ledgers of immaterial wealth. Yet knowledge was convertible into goods as early as the day of the slave-teachers. Education was considered proper for later priesthoods and useful for princes, especially when combined with Machiavellian talent for power. As a refinement of knowledge combined with manners, culture decorated, even when it did not distinguish, several centuries of gentlemen who wore their schooling with a difference (which only in its degeneration was translated into fake university accents and fancy old-school ties).

Only in recent times—but not merely by the development of recent technology—has education been related immediately, solidly, and conspicuously to real wealth in society. The healthy economic condition of this state's society depends not only upon common participation of Texans in educational development within the state but also upon the general recognition of the fact that the Texan, individually and generically, is part of national and international communities of intellectual ideas and cultural resources. Pursuit of truth, defense of freedom, preservation of cultural values—these are not private undertakings. Private opinion and individual independence are made sterile by isolationism; they are starved by educational moats and Chinese walls crossing the cultural world.

Yet too many theories of cultural development have confused isolation with integrity. In Texas, recent years have brought both mixture and conflict, both contact and friction among various mentalities and purposes. Stereotypes of unbridled, uncurried, and uncompromising Texans sufficient unto themselves and vigorously contemptuous of everything not like themselves grew from a misunderstanding of the defense mechanism of the frontier. That mechanism was the most convenient means for fending off the supercilious critic. It generated wildly extravagant Texas reports on everything from weather to dress. All were designed to impress and silence the sophisticated and the effete newcomer, who advertised his superiority by what he wore, what he said, and the way he said it.

Original tall tales and belittling reports were defense mechanisms. It was inevitable that a wide and lively commercial trade in such accounts should end in bad satire about big-hatted Texans on the loose in the cultural capitals of the world and in bad novels about Texans at home.

None of this lore was damaging until it was taken seriously. It became most damaging when Texans, who started it all as a joke, began to take some of it seriously themselves. In the lore that joined its dollar wealth and its intellectual development, Texas lived out a vivid paradox that must be left to the social psychologists. For many years before the Civil War, and for many years after, the state was land-big and dirt-poor. Throughout this period, from about 1846 to 1916, educational activities in Texas were bold and decisive and educational plans so ambitious as to require both the hardihood and the gambling spirit of the frontier. It was after this era that Texas wealth, power, and influence grew.

Texas resources suddenly meant something more than wide expanse of land and wild extremes of temperature. Yet in this new age, educational progress slowed. Sometimes it came to a dead stop. In the era of its biggest boom and its loudest boasts, Texas has not maintained its original self-esteem or its first ambition in things intellectual, cultural, and artistic.

Where were the resolution, sensitive state pride, knowledgeable sense of value, willingness to take a risk, determination to capitalize on the American future in recent decades of compromising on educational minimums, concession to difficulty and deficit? For more than half a century Texas education has needed the same resourcefulness as Texas projects for drilling holes for oil and water, shoving ship channels, plowing the earth, and planing the air.

The irony is doubled now that knowledge has become quickly convertible into cold cash. In modern industry, with growing research budgets, charges for intellection are rapidly overtaking charges for management. Whoever said "A penny for your thoughts" wasn't talking business with an engineer, physicist, or chemist at current rates for scientific consultation in Texas.

Meanwhile, economic and social interrelations of "resources" have grown more and more complex. Time was when raw resources determined the location of an industrial plant. Sometimes these resources still do; but the location committee will also take into elaborate consideration the climate, educational facilities for children, recreational and cultural advantages. Not long ago a distinguished physicist refused to join a company—not because he disliked the salary scale, promotion rate, fringe benefits, and retirement plan but because there was no symphony orchestra within easy driving distance of the plant.

The importance of the mind's production obliges us to a new kind of selectivity and tolerance. We must discount the dull, trite, and pompous; we must encourage the inventive and creative (even when the creative may be restive, rebellious, and damaging to our opinions of ourselves).

By many vivid developments of science and by ingenious adaptations of scientific method in fields that were once thought to be the exclusive province of the homily, anecdote, or editorial guess, we are brought new assurances of certainty in our consideration of educational resources.

In the midst of such blessings we must now remind ourselves that some things still cannot be measured. Quantitative method has not sufficed for painting, though some canvases may be bought by the square inch. Books cannot be encompassed by any mensuration except the uneven and often unequal processes of criticism and bibliography. Quantification of the unquantifiable can lead to a figurative economics of culture more damaging than the old rhetoric of culture that produced the tall tales.

From our present atomic budgets we move back and forth, to and from the educational constitutions contemporary with Ashbel Smith. Perspectives of Texas education, however, are no longer merely historical. Our real history is the continuum that makes all that is conservable about the pioneer state contemporary with Texas culture as it may be forecast for the year 2000. A broad overview of Texas resources suggests some possibilities of our future.

Texas is ideally situated globally, internationally, and nationally to take advantage of the main characteristic of a new educational age: intellect in motion. Texas is no longer an outpost but a crossroads for this intellect. Its educational concerns in fields as various as scientific experiment, economic planning, philosophic discourse, the collection of knowledge, and the creative processes of the arts must be widened. As wide as the human condition and as far-reaching as the prospect of humankind, the Texas stake in this new education must be defined.

This state, among fifty, is best situated to become the focal point of international education. Geographic location is supported by the historical and cultural development of Texas. The symbols of multiple flags that grace the new buildings in Austin now dedicated to Texas history are not mere architectural decorations. The memory and the vitality of the Republic are not sentimental leftovers from an accident of political history. The traditions of hospitality and independence, mixed in Texas experience, are ideally suited to an age that is wringing its hands about world evidence of change, the sort of change that is an old story at our borders.

Texas history has readied this state to take advantage of the challenges of a new era, in which opportunities and obligations are infinitely greater than problems, pitfalls, and disadvantages. Texas is ready to make new history in the institutional dynamics of education. A new educational economics of growth is necessary if it is to live up to the kind of educational progress that was forecast by its past.

Education and the Electric Clock

Texas Quarterly, Autumn 1959

NOT long ago the electric-clock system that times the class periods in a newly constructed university building went awry. After some professional consternation, some student glee, and many bad quotations from *Hamlet*, a new fact about the local chronological measurement of education appeared. Building custodians, professors, and university officials of other stripes and titles were helpless to set clock hands swinging and bells ringing again. The clocks are not owned by the institution. On lease, they must be repaired by agents of the owners. No repairman being available locally, a technician had to be imported from a distance to put the educational process in joint once more. Meanwhile, the building was a kind of educational chaos in miniature. There may be better symbols of our abandonment to the mechanical clocking of education. That one will do.

This is no complaint against machines. It is not a nostalgic appeal to the slow academic days of circles and shadowed angles, those sundials which announced to succeeding generations: "It is later than you think." It is useless to bemoan the merciless motion in time made by the red sweep hand of the electric clock set upon academic measurement. College clocks are a convenience and a contribution to order. What they may signify, however, is another matter.

Ideas of astronomical time and universal time have changed in this century. Once more we are in the midst of a major adjustment of human imagination, as the aerosciences, especially astronautics, shift the ranges of our perspective. In the southwestern United States this shift is particularly notable because it is made against a background of new popular understanding of geological time. Partly because of the oil industry and the consequent influences of the earth sciences, two generations have come to connect our little point in time with the dug past. Conditions in time of the earth's fire, mineral, ice, and water would now be included by any sensible person in any broad attempt to understand the human condition. Geological time is one of the basic concepts of a liberal education.

More recently, big glass eyes and the atomic clocks have made Americans as glib about "light-years" as once they were about the timetables of overland trains, which established in the nation's thinking the once controversial concept of Standard Time. The new dimension of the physicist and the mathematician has come out of the learned monographs into popular communication, however superficial and inaccurate that communication may be. As a consequence, we face changes in the imaginative process much more revolutionary than the historic transition from Ptolemaic to Copernican systems.

Meanwhile, time has become an insistent burden of interpretation and reinterpretation to the historian, whether he is a journalist assigned to "do the story" of America at mid-century or the wide-minded amateur trying to make sense of "historic periods" or "cycles" or epigrammatical turns of phrases like "history repeats itself."

Compared with human-historical time, economic time is apparently more literal. The hour of labor submits to mathematics more easily than to human negotiation between employer and employee when each looks upon it as a negotiable commodity. In our own age, concepts like the forty-hour week have been made and unmade. The eight-hour day, with varying connotations, has provided subjects for sermons, legislation, and community organization. Now speculation puts the three-day week as a probability in the future just ahead and leaves to that future the social problems arising from it.

The time of our life—say, threescore years and ten—has brought the science of geriatrics to maturity. To most of us, biometrics seems to be a curious numbers game, not a profound science by mathematicians by way of sociology, psychology, and economics. To middle-aged pollyannas, life still begins at forty, however loudly biochemists and biophysicists declare that man begins to die a score of years before that. To capitalize on shifts in the chronological center of population, old-age clubs have been made a political bonanza; but none of this riddling with the life span can avoid the enormous social and psychological implication of the fact that man—generic man—supported by antibiotics and other instruments of modern sciences, is living later and later while his society is rejecting him as a working member earlier and earlier.

For what it is worth, this new biometric emphasis has at least interested the English-speaking world in the living conditions of old age. Witness our present eager emphasis on retirement. This emphasis has itself produced astonishing new perspectives on human lifetime. For simpler if less comfortable notions of thrift and planning, we have substituted ideals of guaranteed security and thereby created falsely advertised concern among Americans in their twenties about what their retirement pay at age seventy will be. Only postwar threats of wars-to-come have wakened us to the intellectual dishonesty of trying to prophesy future economic conditions.

Thus, by universal view, by rearview mirrors toward the past, by long-span conditions of living, time has affected the intellectual, philosophical, legislative, and social views of Americans in our era. Yet our attitudes toward the element of time in education have not kept up with these great developments.

Attitudes toward "our" year, considered as a condition of living or as one of an essential group of personal resources, show the tenseness that invades our sense of the calendar. Abandoning the ease of natural seasons, we long ago imposed the neatly dissected year, slicing our time at ten dozen cutting points dictated by fashions, sports, vacations, and other observances more ritual-istic than primitive tribal customs and ten times more deadly to the spirit struggling for a free existence in time.

The month submits to the same kind of tyranny, rearranged into all kinds of unnatural patterns. Even more tense, to a degree nearly neurotic, are attitudes toward "our" day, our sense of the clock. Some time ago, the easy spaces of sunshine and moonshine, workday and rest time, were abolished by lining off wakeful hours into fifteen-minute halting stops.

In college life the most obvious difficulties and some of the less obvious tyrannies arise from the solemn attempts to measure educational experience by mere duration. There is, first, the nine-month year, an educational shackle worn lightly by those who think they need a three-month vacation from a "fifteen-hour schedule" in a "four-year degree program" embracing a carefully clocked 120- or 130- or 136-hour "degree."

Let us pay sincere respect to all arms of the educational organization that administer the arithmetical-chronological ritual, including, especially, long-suffering registrars. Let us also respect the ingenuity and wit of the undergraduate "catalogue lawyer," who by zeal not given to many in our community—not even to senior members of the faculty—reads the elaborated requirements so carefully that he is able to extend a three-hour credit to cover a four-hour deficit or who avoids a six-hour condition by trotting out some "unquantitated" experience like a forty-five–day correspondence course or a four-year stint as navigator in one of the armed forces and thus (one whole semester before schedule) becomes officially educated—that is, the possessor of a bachelor's degree.

This is not to suggest that the quantitation which is not really quantitative should be abolished. Even those of us who oppose the "credit system" do not propose to abandon it—yet—because none of us has hit upon a workable substitute. But just as we resist vain and destructive attacks upon this academic chronocracy, let us not avoid the necessity of recognizing and branding it for what it is: a ritual, at best convenient or necessary and at worst capable of killing the purposes of higher education in the individual.

Let us also recognize the fact that our educational system must
continue to accommodate a tremendous number of important future adult citizens who for various social reasons cannot be (and
for various social reasons should not be) submitted to a system
purely quantitative. We make our first great error by consenting
to treat education as a series of timed exercises instead of a continuous development. We make our second great error in assuming that somehow "adult education" is separated in the learning
process. This phrase is a useful one, and we cannot do without it.
But we should not use it apologetically as a label to describe something slightly eccentric. Newspaper accounts make it quite clear
that the American public considers adults somewhat odd when
they go on with their formal education after they have passed the
decent time for it. Yet it is surely an error to assume that one ever
reaches a point in time when education is not proper to him as a
human being. It is unperceptive to assume that universities should
not mix "college education" with "adult education." It is educa-
tionally unsound because it can be psychologically damaging to
the student as well as wasteful to society.

The turn-on and shut-off processes of timing in our educational
institutions are worse than distracting to the person who launches
himself upon the continuous process of learning. Shut off elementary education, turn on high school, shut off high school, turn on
college, shut off college, turn on law or medicine or graduate
study or (as the advertisements say with a sort of left-handed
damnation of the whole educational system) turn on "real life."

Everywhere fixation upon time as the iron-handed, lead-headed
god of education boxes us. We stand amazed and pedagogically
all thumbs before the child of ten who has learned to read and who
remembers what he reads or the child of ten who has learned to
figure and delights in figuring. The most serious embarrassments
of our educational system are these students who get an education
faster than the clock turns, who inconvenience us by upsetting
our neat pedagogical calendars.

For these and all other students, American education needs
highly individual continuity of the learning process. To this need

of continuity, one must add immediately the equally important need of a wise judgment of values. There is a necessary discrimination between the timely and the timeless in education. Nobody would deny the uses of mere modernity in college training. But nobody who has the slightest respect for education would ignore the fact that modernity offers both promises and pitfalls. Educated Americans should be capable of conducting decent burials for what is intellectually dead and deadening. By the same process (although one changes the figure to describe the judgment) they should be capable of installing the new discovery, of hailing new proofs, of welcoming the new surmise—even the wild one.

All this has to do with timed education. To whatever philosophy of time the real student submits himself, by whatever quality of harrowed deadline or wide-rolling eternity he governs his selections of what will make his education, he needs a plan that runs counter to time. He needs to have a proper respect for untimed learning, even if he cannot himself rejoice in it. He needs to recognize the fact that some men, though perhaps not he, must be mainly concerned with engagements of the spirit while the concerns of others tick nervously on and on until the electricity finally is shut off. Among fine sentiments of what his education got him he needs to scribble down somewhere that at one time leisure and scholarship were joined, in the same word. He should be able to recognize in untimed learning, in "unquantitated study," the gradual maturing of wisdom. He may be wise enough to know that he really failed the course for which he has *A* credit and that in the course which by quantitation gave him only "three hours of *C*" he nevertheless advanced the boundaries of his spirit. He will always respect the high academic record for the least it can be—a quantitative score that the student makes in his tactics against ignorance. But he will also respect the strategy of the educated man who knows how to waste time, joyfully and to good effect. He will also know that the clock is not sufficient for the man whose perspective must take into account the past and whose vision must reckon with the future.

Students in the Singular

Address, Honors Day, Southern Methodist University, 1957*

I F students and faculties everywhere could agree about any one thing, it would be that grades should be abolished. They will be abolished only when somebody finds a better means of keeping academic records and measuring academic accomplishment. If one ignores their market value and prophetic significance, good grades are sound reason for congratulation because, if nothing more, they reflect the ability and willingness of the student to meet the rules of academic competition and to pay intelligent attention to mental business, to the educational responsibilities he assumes of his own free will.

My main argument has to do with students in the singular. Although we live by an educational theory that is focused on the individual, most of the recent discussion of American education has been devoted to students in the mass. This is true in part because in the years just ahead the educational system must somehow accommodate huge numbers of students. Hence figures of speech like "floods of undergraduates," "tidal waves of freshmen," and other rhetoric implying that in large numbers students become some kind of tremendous natural disaster.

The simple truth is that, just as our crafts turned into industry and learned mass production, education will have to learn something of mass production in its turn; otherwise, we will deny advanced training to large numbers of younger citizens. Some of the

* Revised versions published by *Phi Kappa Phi Journal*, 1961; *Daily Texan*, 1961; and *UT Record*, 1961.

advantages of mass production are obvious. We can make plans for educating large armies of college people only by assuming that groups of them—the abstract "sophomore" or the theoretical "pre-law," "pre-med," "theology," or "business" student—constitute figures definite enough for us to describe a degree to fit them or to frame a course for them or to devise metes and bounds in which they can labor or relax. At the same time we must be sure that we do not damage their chances of remaining individuals while they become educated Americans.

Technology has given us more mechanic assistance in education than punched cards for registration records and microfilm for reducing those records to a kind of plastic immortality. By associating techniques we can even make the technology of educational mass production provide new kinds of highly individualized study, the developments that are being lumped under the term "do-it-yourself education."

The real danger in mass production comes when our habits of describing masses of students or abstract types (and our encouraging students to think of themselves in these terms) are allowed to govern our whole system. Then something called Adjustment takes the place of Education. Sooner or later we allow infringements upon the individual student's conscience, taste, legitimate aspiration, or time. All this adjusting to type and mass-production schedule is sensible provided it does not rob the student of his rights or does not diminish his responsibilities, obligations, and potentialities, which are much more important to the individual's education than his rights. In processing and adjusting, in massing and molding, we have accomplished wonders. We have also encouraged too many students, including honor students, to dread being "different," as if intellectual differences were a kind of educational cancer.

It would pay us if we stopped in the educational process more often to remember that there are various kinds of differing among intelligent human beings. Some kinds are indeed malignant. Like cancer, they grow wild-cell minds and personalities. Even worse, some kinds of eccentricity, standardized in idiotic group mores, actually destroy the value of the group because they make that group signify only foolishness or wastefulness or meaninglessness or evil. But there are other differings and eccentricities that are benignant. The student in the singular has a great many legitimate mass demands to meet; he also has his singular integrity and honor, his own intellectual ideals that must be pursued and sustained for his healthy growth. Human beings, one and many, thrive on such differences. A man will not be less capable of suiting the mold of law, medicine, theology, real estate, or teaching because he insists on maintaining his individual design of life. Any profession that consents to a stereotype for its members is dead, for it has denied the life-principle of change.

But the distinction between group and individual values is not the sort of either-or proposition that extremists on both sides would have us believe. In sum, education should always preserve this student in the singular while it advances his power to act as an effective member of his group.

Because I am now going to say some strong words about freedom of students in the singular, I am compelled to preface the statement by an obvious fact. Those who believe in the intellect know that there is no freedom more satisfying, none more complete, than the liberty of the well governed. There is no personal freedom so great as that which results from self-discipline. There is no educational waste so costly as intellectual anarchy.

Having made that undeniable preface, I would argue the cause of students who are self-propelled and self-directed and who are learning to rejoice in the enlivening uncertainty of cultivated intellect. Such students, learning the cost of good self-government and the wisdom that can grow out of error, create natural habits of hospitable tolerance. They do not have to live on academic tranquilizing pills or be doped into stupefied happiness. They never accept the insult of easeful and ready-made education.

They are prepared for change. They are aware that the habit of solving every problem by asking others simply denies them capacity for thinking and living. They are resolutely capable of making critical inventories, including critical inventories of themselves.

By these expressed signs in the individual we distinguish the student singular from herds that move like driven cattle. The student who is herded gives up his role as a rational human being.

In order to fill this role effectively the individual student should look to certain freedoms. The first is freedom from empty tradition. Few experiences are more deadening to the alert mind than having to follow a path simply because it is well beaten. By such academic mortmain the real values that education is designed to preserve get crusted with useless formalism. The truth that each student is supposed to pursue is lost in a wilderness of pip-squeak observances, empty wise-saws, and outmoded methods.

Second, the singular student should be free from slavedom to mere utility. Whoever goes into a career or a college course merely for utilitarian advantage will certainly achieve nothing beyond utilitarian advantage. Nor will his education be sufficient for understanding and enjoying even that.

A third liberty that our student, acting as a singular member of the academic world, must seek is freedom from mere fad. "It has always been done" is a lazy argument. "It pays" is a short-sighted one. But "It is the fashionable thing to do" appeals only to the mindless, the very dim of wit, those who are too shallow to judge tradition wisely and too shifty of mind to welcome new values intelligently.

Our singular student should also be free from casual academic opinion. There is more offhand advice available in the academic world than in any other sphere of human existence. Some of it makes sense. Some of it makes sense only for some people.

The most important freedom that we should guarantee to our individual student is his freedom to make mistakes. Most disturbing is the person who has undertaken the temporary job of being a serious student and who does not realize the tremendous value of negative results. Until a student has learned what it is to "labor to no use," until he has discovered the importance of failing and assessing the failure, he has not even begun to prepare himself for the realities of life, he has not become a member of the human race. The human being is peculiar among animals in making greatest sense of its apparent failures, in capitalizing on its disasters.

If any of these convictions be true, one deep conviction follows inevitably. Every individual student, acting in the singular, will discover that his beliefs (as distinguished from the wisdom, knowledge, or skill on which he makes examination grades) will shape him, the believer; they are the unavoidable instruments of his living—any kind of living. They are unavoidable and they are essential in a true educational community.

The Rediscovery of Teaching

Texas Quarterly, Winter 1965

M ANY Americans have been cheered—and some have been chastened—by recent clamor about teaching. First a loud chorus, not yet silent, brought a series of indictments against the present state of undergraduate instruction. Behind the negative rhetoric there were hard negative facts. The "flight from teaching" was illustrated by numerous faculty members departing the campus for industrial and federal appointments. More disturbing were statistics within the university: larger budgets invited larger numbers of the faculty to do less teaching in order to do more research. "Publish or perish" policies, sometimes exaggerated or misunderstood, seemed to sound a death knell for the teacher's historic concern with students. Student outcry, which once had been spontaneous expression of the undergraduate's inalienable right to complain, changed tone. Students put their case in forceful terms: they objected less to what and how they were being taught (an ancient complaint) than to the fact that some were sure they were being completely ignored (a new and serious charge).

Quickly the press and the public rediscovered the importance of teaching. The Sputnik syndrome, which had roused insistent, incoherent demands for research, invention, innovation, and technology persisted. National defense sustained it. It was next overlapped, however, by nostalgia for the teacher, ready and eager to teach, facing a ready and eager learner.

Querulousness and questioning signified more than natural

prudence and pedagogical nostalgia. Old arguments revived familiar testy questions. Is today's student really learning? Is the student really being brought forward to responsible independence? Are students really moving toward high goals? If not, what does the university propose to do about it?

For some time now, the United States has been holding a wide-flung town meeting on such matters. Confusing though some of the arguments may be, surely this involvement of public, press, and academic community in common purposes is healthy. More than that, it enlivens tradition and defines opportunity. Educators cannot avoid or escape this hubbub. Very few would choose to do so.

During this period we learned a whole vocabulary of educational pessimism: "dropout," "campus revolutionaries," "late bloomer," "college illiterates." We also learned about new theories of learning, new arenas of teaching (auditoriums, laboratories, libraries), new educational aids (television, information retrieval, publication and communication devices).

To both deficiencies and demands for improvement we must first bring the common heritage of the university world. Then we must resort to common sense. From the time when Socrates was younger than Macaulay's schoolboy, learners have been education's main asset. If an educational renaissance is under way, it is largely because of revitalized concern about these learners. For one thing, there are so many of them. Their numbers will continue to increase. In ways not apparent to earlier generations, they are now interested in what happens to their own minds. Some of them are also concerned about the social issues of knowledge, about what may happen later to a world they must inherit and can, perhaps, remake.

New avenues opened by sudden and self-interested preoccupation with research should not be discounted. The results should be discouraged only when they are irrelevant, futile, or fake. It was a good explosion. Let us give equal emphasis to the academic implosion by which forces have rushed into temporary emptiness at the teaching center.

In our longer academic deliberations it has been necessary constantly to emphasize the inseparable connections between teaching and research. It is still necessary, although the fact is not generally accepted. Apart from a university's obligation to search the unknown and face the unknowable, great research is an important kind of great teaching. Published research is naked exposure of one or more minds to other minds. In education no process is more candid, none more rigorous in communicating knowledge.

We have all made long lists of curriculum experiments, evaluation and reevaluation systems, and such devices as "teaching teams" (a platoon offense inspired in part by the success of research teams). We have noted with gratification that budgets reflect the results of our semesters of discontent: teaching awards, grants for teaching improvement, emphasis upon classroom effectiveness as a criterion for advancement of the faculty, plans for recruiting able instructors of undergraduates.

The teaching was always there to be done. During the lowest ebb of emphasis upon it, there were always those not only willing but also determined to share that responsibility and to risk going unrewarded. With a new upsurge of support for this phase of university work, what now? What next?

Among our prospects, there are pitfalls. We will not solve future problems by resort to formulas, hard and fast systems, or aimless imitation and adaptation of what seems successful on some distant campus. At the outset I would suggest emphasis on two general facts sometimes forgotten.

— The youngest university student (a freshman or a sophomore) is registered in three to five or more courses conducted as quite distinct if not completely unrelated processes of learning. Meanwhile, his instructors, rightly concerned with the blinders of specialty, usually suffer from current underexposure to other academic disciplines. The undergraduate, of course, is expected to acquire, retain, and relate the whole array of miscellaneous instruction.

— There is a practical fallacy in the *A-B-C-D* method of measuring attainment. If an undergraduate completes a course with a grade of 75, or *C*, he may conclude that he knows only three-fourths of what he was supposed to learn. Worse, he may assume that 25 percent of his effort went to failure or futility. Yet, as a matter of experience, he may have got twice as much as he was supposed to get. Regardless of his grade, later significance of what he did get may shrink to zero or expand to vast proportions. Some knowledge takes months or years in fusing. That knowledge may fizzle. It may burst into new wisdom. A recent survey asked one thousand alumni graduated in the thirties to evaluate classroom experience. The replies showed clearly that estimates of significance had little to do with grades. Almost 40 percent of the high-value marks were given courses in which the alumnus had made *C* or less.

Frustration about definitions of good teachers and good teaching is misleading, for it implies greater difficulty than practical experience warrants. This avowed uncertainty is a natural response of the most self-critical profession in the world, a profession that once circled among its private doubts but now confronts a vocal, aggressive, ambitious, and worried clientele. The problem has been magnified by advertisements of campus woes and ignorance of campus accomplishments. In any event, the following reminders should be mixed with resolutions:

—Good teachers are not uniformly and invariably effective with all students.

—From department to department, criteria of good teaching may vary; and only on small, homogeneous campuses can they be uniformly applied.

—In transition from secondary education to the college level and in later transitions through college to graduate study and post-doctoral work, the teaching function must change if only because its purpose changes.

—To sustain good teaching and to improve it, some kind of sensible and generally acceptable method of evaluation is necessary. Apart from primary requisites of intelligibility and acceptability, it must combine principle with practice of adaptability in particular cases. The principle is simple justice. The adaptability is required by the fact that both teachers and their evaluators are human beings: so far no machine or statistical method has been quite equal to the task.

— Evaluation by colleagues ("peers" as the surveys call them) brings to bear the necessary professional competence, mingled with other random human elements.

— Evaluation by alumni provides more than perspective in time; it can reflect the staying power as well as the hitting power of instruction.

— Evaluation by students is not new and has never been systematic. Complicating the judgment of undergraduates by elaborate sampling and comparative numerical analysis will not systematize the results. Such evaluation is important if only for its own sake. Its importance is doubled when the course is evaluated along with the instructor.

— Evaluation by more objective means (standard examinations, academic consultants, professional critics) can be effective only if the process is clear to the teacher and to his department and if it is prevented from becoming routine or desultory.

— At many points in the university world, some combination of these methods is already used. The most neglected possibility is the most obvious one: assessment of his teaching by the instructor himself. It should always be joined with one or more other devices. If the instructor thinks he is effective but isn't, the department has a problem. If the instructor thinks he is ineffective and all the evidence confirms his opinion, he has a serious problem and the department has only one course of action, unpleasant to all concerned. But if the instructor thinks his teaching needs improvement when he is obviously effective in the classroom, he should be cherished.

—Since the art of teaching is in short supply and academic tenure is of long duration, questions of change rise once more. Like students, teachers develop in different ways. A good teacher one year may become a poor one later, especially if he is caught up in the delusions of popularity or the laziness of repeating the same old success. On the other hand, an ineffective teacher may find by deliberate experiment, by determined slow effort, and by any number of accidents (including the not uncommon one of spontaneous encouragement from students themselves) that real effectiveness is just beyond the next registration.

In most discussions of teaching, the word *learning* is used too little. After his last commencement is adjourned, the student will still have easy access to formal education: adult courses, special courses, lectures. Nevertheless, if he has not proved the uses of learning by himself, on his own impulse, he will have missed the most important lesson his university can teach him.

In this sector of education, we have made some progress. Directed study programs, honors courses, and tutorial systems have been joined lately by undergraduate research programs, awards for creative work outside courses, and numerous plans for solo study in reading periods, summer vacations, and spare time. Formal encouragement has been given such activity by the advanced-standing examination.

Still needed, however, are much larger budgets to provide much wider opportunities. Above all, such independent work should be recognized more widely, even when, at first glance, it seems to be obtuse as well as independent. Thoreau's distant drummer is still drumming; but too many academic ears catch only a sound muffled by curriculum requirements, grades, counsel to safety, and stuffy habits acquired through secondhand experience.

For the successful teacher, his job is a joy. It is also hard, never-ending work. In this respect, we must keep repeating that the laborer is worthy of his hire, and something else: he is worthy of time to renew his perspective, restore his power, update what he knows, and, above all, pay some attention to the darkling plains of his own ignorance in an intellectual world that still marks much of the vast academic map "incognita."

Whoever he is, wherever he is, the teacher faces a new day, professionally and socially. Very few prophets have been so honored in their own country by alternating acclaim and distrust, applause and suspicion. Unusual attention has brought the usual conflicting results—self-confidence and insecurity, satisfaction in feeling part of the American mainstream and realization that helping to shape the future is not a task that can be undertaken in the comfortable obscurity of library, laboratory, or classroom. Somehow I doubt that this condition would have astonished teachers who lived in an earlier, much more tumultuous time and understood the relationship of education to a democratic society.

Teaching and Research

Texas Quarterly, Spring 1958

AMONG academic questions none has generated more confusion or aroused more idle controversy than the relationship between teaching and research in the university community. For some members of that community, not among the least wise, the question is academic in more than one sense of the term. Personal experience has convinced them that the widely reported conflict between research and teaching is often imaginary and in any case needless. They believe that neat distinctions among terms, like prolonged discussion of the issue, avail nothing; so they live happily in a union of research with teaching.

Not all members of the academic community, however, attain this state of felicity. Some who work at the problem in varying degrees of discomfort feel that they would not be plagued by it if the university system of rank and salary, appointment and promotion, were not involved. Others accept this system in theory but complain that its administrative operation as related to teaching and research is either arbitrary or completely inscrutable. Consequent feelings concerning injustice, misdirection, and mixed value make the whole issue a "cause," and to that cause many able men and women devote more of their emotions and energy than either the abstract problem or the practical effect upon academic fortunes warrants.

One thing is clear at the start. Except for those rare—and rarely distinguished—institutions that follow a single purpose and a completely uniform academic process, an organized faculty is not a nice arrangement of round and square pegs and holes. The dynamics of a university must come from differences, from differences that keep changing and that can be adjusted only temporarily. Whatever unity a university attains must be attained in this changing variety of opinion, conviction, hypothesis, and proof. This principle is as applicable to professors themselves as it is to the academic program and to those approximations of truth which the academic program is established to examine and to communicate.

Recognition of these conditions does not require the proclamation of easy relativism or mere anarchy. It leads almost invariably to a consideration of cases. It usually leads to extreme cases, for they are easiest to describe and are often the source of warm argument. In an academic democracy, extremes are due sympathetic and respectful consideration, even when they cannot be accommodated easily—or at all.

Professor A has intellectual gifts and great competence in the practice of research (the two are not identical). He does not dislike people; he does not dislike very young beginners in learning; he does not underestimate the social and academic importance of the "communication of ideas." But he heartily dislikes teaching, or the only kind of teaching open to him during the first ten or fifteen years of his career. Almost inevitably, then, he becomes a "research man." He beats no unsteady retreat into the library or the laboratory; he marches in, nose forward, and takes a firm stand at the point in the university where he can follow his own bent, as free as possible from the uncongenial labors of the lecture hall, the conference office, and the committee assignment. Any one of these would distract him from what is singularly important to him and what, he rightly believes, is essential to his university: the advancement of knowledge.

Thus removed from common labors, standing symbolic and dedicated to the learning of the time, Professor A is not subject to our argument. Indeed, the most trivial-minded critic considers him an academic adornment, and those who are seriously concerned with higher education know that he and his purposes are at the very center of the university. There would be no future university without him, for teaching cannot proceed exclusively upon what we have learned in the past; and a university cannot pretend to its title unless it contributes something to what all universities may teach in the future.

Professor B is a different man. He begins with endowments not easy to distinguish from Professor A's gifts. He produces, bona fide, a sound piece of research, whereupon he neither retreats nor takes up a stand in library or laboratory. Instead, by canny reconnoitering, he discovers that rewards of publication are fast and impressive, especially in fields that happen to be in wide demand among industries, federal programs, or private philanthropies. He resolves to make the best of a good thing. Perhaps in alternate and less cynical moods he merely subsides, letting his dedication to the cause of learning slide into comfortable assurance brought on by the discovery of a little fact. He lives on his early laurels—a rich diet even if his field is esoteric and in demand almost nowhere. From one foray into the backwoods of knowledge he has returned with a discovery. Now he can begin a cycle of "articles." He may even get a book, varying somewhat the method or even the results of the articles. If he can get no second book, he can always revise the first after a decent interval.

Professor C is an extreme among extremes. He is not given to research, but against nature he gives himself to it anyway. He knows that the production of notes, abstracts, and inconsequential reviews constitutes "publication." Allowed sufficient time at the normal rate of annual accretion, they make a bibliography at last. So he proceeds to grind, with a spirit akin to that of his colleague in the next office who goes to an MWF class at 10:00 only because the chairman has assigned him the class on MWF at 10:00. After five notes and six book reviews, he gets a research leave during which he compiles a "study," by virtue of which he is recommended for advancement because he has "done research." He then applies for a printing grant, and when the printing grant has been spent on printing, he is recommended for advancement again because, undeniably, he has "published." There is some doubt about the value of his publication, but there is no doubt about its quantity. His promotion may result from a system that cannot always tell (because sometimes only time can tell) true excellence in research.

These cases—A, B, and C—are not to be confused with the larger body academic. Yet such extremes, ranging from a kind of intellectual chivalry to plain educational chicanery, obscure the true significance of research to the academic community. Fortunately, the vast majority of professors competent to do research are not so fired by their genius that they must burn forever upward to a point of blissful obliviousness of the rest of society. Nor are the majority impelled to trade on shallow pretenses at learning or empty results of makeshift investigation. To this majority, research is always closely connected with their teaching and often inseparable from it.

Indeed, research is a kind of teaching, one of the several means by which the academic world communicates facts and ideas, by which curiosity and the further growth of knowledge are stirred, and by which in the long, slow, total process human wisdom may be increased. There is no teaching—not by the scintillant lecturer who holds rows and rows of students breathless, nor by the sympathetic counselor counseling ever so wisely—there is no teaching at all that can compare with the experience of the student who is allowed to follow at close quarters a great research worker at his desk.

What of that teaching which, for purposes of defining the academic day or the professor's load, must be considered separately from research? What of that academic work which cultivates habits of study instead of advancing knowledge, is occupied with communication instead of discovery? This teaching, like research, produces in every university certain exceptions to the general rule and certain offenses against the golden mean.

Professor L, for example, has been excited to teach by having experienced the unique elation of the learning process and by identifying the cause of his intellectual pleasure with a great teacher. He is intelligent in the best sense: his mind grasps, selects, rejects, retains. For him teaching becomes not merely giving and giving and giving but a process of growth, a kind of

growth less obvious, it is true, than that of the researcher who
strides across marked and publicly notable boundaries of knowledge. Just as the best possible research man inevitably teaches, so
the best possible teacher must conduct research in order to sustain
his teaching. As often as not, however, this teacher talks about
his ideas until he changes them, and in the changing makes publication impossible or unnecessary. He does not write books and
articles and notes and reviews as a regular part of his week or
year. Occasionally, he does write something, however, unworried
by the fact that what he writes is more readable than memorable.

Professor M begins with clear ideals and practical plans for his
own education and for the education of others. Little by little he
compromises his early standard, excusing his compromise with
argument about serving more students. Soon he contends that the
generalization of knowledge is more important than specialization (whereupon he begins to collect jokes about specialists). Or
he publicly defends the "human" against the "impersonal" ap-
proach (and begins to cultivate the charms of learning instead of
its severities). Or he simply asserts that a university is, after all
and above all, a teaching institution. So he finds reasons enough
for postponing—if he is decisive, for abandoning—research. Still
he clings to serious study because he is too intelligent and too well
trained to live happily very long without it.

Professor N does not complete this roll, but he will do to bring
any academic alphabet to a halt. He has entered teaching because
he thinks the job a pleasant one. He soon discovers that its pleasures are vastly exaggerated by those who associate pleasure with
idleness and idleness with professorship. The burdens of serious
teaching are too much for him; with imprecations upon the "teaching load," he finds means of unloading. He cultivates all sorts of
irrelevance, omission, and substitution. He devotes himself to
"just talking about the subject," a way of saying nothing. He professes vast concern for casual undergraduate activities and individual preoccupations of students, who usually manage such matters better without elderly assistance. He may bring sincere
friendliness and kindness into the classroom world, but that world

is already so kind to undergraduates that it is likely to give many of them ill preparation for later life.

The rest of the alphabet could provide other types and single out rare individuals who crop up in education here and there, laws unto themselves, defying both definition and imitation.

The real issue here, of course, is one common in many moral contexts—not what to think about it, but what to do about it. Serious thought on the subject has produced numerous devices and methods for the evaluation of teaching and research. The most common process of evaluation is the simplest: judgments, successive or cumulative, registered by administrative officials responsible for departments, divisions, areas, schools, and colleges. To fertilize these judgments, ad hoc committee reports, drawn from within the university faculty or from outside sources, are being required more and more widely. To add special evidence, statistics, personal opinions of those who have been taught, and surveys (of grading, of scholarly reviews, of comparative productivity) are often introduced; and so are "opinionnaires" (a device for making subjective attitudes scientific by means of writing them down and counting them).

Among so many earnest attempts to do well and to do justice, two points are commonly neglected. One is a source of opinion, the other a manifest but easily forgotten fact. The academician can often throw light on his own work, and we need better means for encouraging him to do so. In many cases the fairest (and in some the severest) tribunal for his accomplishment will be self-evaluation, made intelligible to those responsible for decisions.

The fact too easily forgotten in all such considerations is that tensions set up between teaching and research in a university are personal, highly complex, and subject to no institutional rules of thumb. Policies and systems should therefore emphasize clarity, fairness, and a resolute sense of values rather than consistency and the illusion of exactness. We are not likely to get far in understanding scholarship in the abstract without insight into scholars in the singular, nor are we likely to see the teaching process clearly unless we can get clearer views of that individualist, the teacher.

Personality and Impersonality in Academic Life

Texas Quarterly, Autumn 1963

WITH all the quiet strategies and polite tactics that occupy the academic world, there has never been a successful revolution against the tyranny of words.

By open disclaimer or silent distrust, we have arrayed ourselves courageously against many other enemies of good academic sense and good educational health. About dangers of slipping up on slick phraseology or falling headlong into pitfalls of academic fustian, we have been content with lame resort to mere definition ("Webster says") or satire on pedagogical jargon, bombast, and double-talk. We have been successful in pointing out that fatuousness is indeed fatuous; but we have not insisted often enough that it can also be costly and damaging.

Rhetoric faces inescapable risks in fields usually better clarified by quantitative study. But sooner or later even the most exact study of academic life works back into a verbal context. In that context we still shape our plans and direct our operations. It will be a greatly simplified academic society when one can compute this and follow the formulas of that. We shall not live to see the day.

Educational rhetoric confronts its greatest burden when it must handle the problems of academic individualism. Educational concern with personality emphasizes the singular human being, considered in his totality, not merely in his mature profession of one area of knowledge or according to his youthful progress toward a college degree. We compare this concern for the individual with the impersonality rising steadily at every increase in enrollment, at every new proliferation of what we call *curricula* in our last sad deference to Latin, and at the erection of various *gymnasia* and *mausolea* for man muscular and man mental.

This impersonality is first of all simply nonanthropic. It often leaves out man completely when it professes greatest interest in him. It is not only nonpersonal; it is often antipersonal, giving the individual a deep—and sometimes a disturbingly sudden—conviction that he must be to all others what he is not and cannot be to himself. This conviction of nonbeing is different from the older conviction of sin, which man found remediable by various devices. Nor is educational nonentity associated with any such state of bliss promised to adherents of certain Oriental beliefs. On the contrary, its final conclusion is inevitable. As one character in a drama has said, nothing shall come of nothing.

Education, by any count, is a long process. At different chronological stages, the academic personality demands different environments. It is too easy to say that the process must accommodate both youth and age. It is plainly foolhardy to assume that the ideal condition of academic life (or the ideal point for observing it) is located approximately midway of a straight life line between post-adolescence and presenility. By sheer multiplicity, individuals in the case will confound any such reasoning.

Today there are two quite different kinds of impersonality on the university campus. The first is the impersonality of those educated men and women who are moved by devotion to scientific method or objective criticism, belief in the value of accuracy, willingness to forego subjective commitment and expression. They deliberately eliminate the merely personal equation from at least some of their academic calculations and activities.

The second is the impersonality of nonpersonal devices, such as the machine, and consequent methods of research, teaching, and administration. There is no question that we have a greater debt to these nonpersonal devices than quantity and speed of operation. Vital statistics, and some statistics that are required but not very vital, come now in the responses of computers responding to highly charged questions about people and peoples. New to us so far, the teaching machines—like an elementary student's Aladdin's slate—should encourage and not douse the enthusiasm of the academics who firmly believe that teaching must at its best be a highly personal activity (but who sometimes ignore the fact that learning, by the very nature of what is learned, must sometimes be completely and intensely impersonal). It is true, I suppose, that some teachers on television resemble nothing more closely than a cross between a salesman and a breakfast-club master of ceremonies. Yet it would take a resolved primitive in education not to welcome the wonders of Telefax simply because the facts don't come grimly inked by hand, laboriously and locally and not very accurately dug up. We are on the verge of a new mining of knowledge, and personality stands to gain, not whimsically as in a fairy tale but sensibly and systematically as in a university it should.

Apart from the merely nonpersonal, there are other impersonalities in academic life. One comes of focusing, not merely altruistically but rationally, on the other point of view, the other person, the other argument. Another comes of extending the person's community of interest, through local and regional and national and international contexts, until what turns full circle brings him to mankind. Still another comes from the wider range of view in time, in place, in conceptual method. Grammar, A. S. Cook once said, is a very intimate thing to a student who really understands it. Nothing is likely to make it more intimate for a student than getting a vague notion of how differently intimate a different kind of grammar can be to a Choctaw or an Eskimo.

Another kind of grammatical experience points to what we call —and miscall—communication in the personal-impersonal tensions of the academic life. Communication among some academic groups becomes involved and difficult for a curious reason. Most sensible people wait to communicate only until they have an idea. For an academic, however, the idea is likely to be only a misty beginning. He must test the idea itself. Then he must select a mode of expression for it. Then he must test that mode. If he is very sensitive he circles back to anticipate its reception, in terms of its various implications for him and the likelihood of different effects upon others. All this is his way of defending against half-baked notions. Too often in this guarding against the precocious, he bakes the idea until it is ash in the pan.

A second handicap to communication is academic delicacy. Nothing brings university antennae to quiver as do such intimate and ticklish questions as assignment, attainment, and advancement of teachers. On more impersonal grounds agitation is about equal when somebody proposes changing a curriculum—almost any curriculum—or doubts the accuracy of a grading system. For students, communication becomes a most delicate matter (which lies at the very heart of any system designed to educate them) when it involves their right to be wrong and to be vociferous about it. This tiptoe attitude toward one another and toward the process of education (indeed, toward what concerns us most and most personally) can be very costly. It is costliest when it subverts that lusty agent of truth, honesty. It is deadliest when it robs us of what learning and teaching still can be, fun.

Administration and organization of "academic personnel" work more smoothly by manipulation of ciphers than they do by figuring in less obedient terms of the individual. Traditionally, the significance of the academic populace has never been even a rough equivalent of its social organization but is still almost exactly the sum of its significant individual members.

Under these terms administrative difficulties in communicating are often unavoidable. They become unendurable only when the dangers peculiar to the lot of an administrator worst his candor and his clarity. The first occupational disease of an administrator sets in when what he must say sticks in his throat, for whatever reason good or bad. Almost as disturbing is the discovery that the iron megaphone inherited from generations of loud proclaimers about education will not do anything but rouse derisive echoes.

When such impersonal equipment distorts both intention and meaning, we are left with simple measures. We will not soon invent amplifying systems and instant communicators to do the job for us. There is, in sum, nothing for it but plain talk. Plain question. Plain answer. And when we don't have the answer—remembering that not all the answers are in—plain admission that, God help us, we are ignorant.

The Arts of Uncertainty

Texas Quarterly, Summer–Autumn 1958*

By what may be called the arts of certitude man has contrived to move, though unsteadily, from point to point in his long pilgrimage. By these arts he has extended his life and multiplied its comforts. By these arts he has made all kinds of things; he has, as we like to say, made progress. Having acquired much knowledge, he has the sense of having acquired some certainty. These are great accomplishments: indeed, they account for most of what the man in the street calls "civilization." Yet, about himself, about his fellowmen, about life, he still confronts much that is vague, changeful, unpredictable, immeasurable, unknown, unknowable. The humanities confront all such things. Compared with the true sciences and with the arts of certitude, compared even with various crafts of profitable doing and workable guessing, the humanities remain the arts of uncertainty.

For generations these arts, translated into academic discipline, have been the object of contradictory social and educational practices. They have roused various kinds of enthusiasm, ranging from genuine devotion to patently hypocritical palaver about "cultural subjects in the curriculum." Before they were sullied by too much lip service, they were more or less central to an education based upon certain assumptions not always tenable in these days. Teach-

* Other versions published in *Alcalde*, 1958, and in *Proceedings*, Bowling Green Conference of National Commission on Teacher Education and Professional Standards, National Education Association, 1958.

ers could once assume, for example, that students were more or less alike: alike in being—or in striving to be—ladies and gentlemen, in aspiring to a responsible citizenship dedicated to keeping social, intellectual, and artistic values intact. Above all, such students of the humanities were assumed to be alike in the impulse to maintain the integrity of their cultural tradition. Part of this tradition was the image of the educated man and woman, figures to be reckoned with in any estimate of those times.

Attitudes toward education change. These attitudes changed. Culture and the tradition of it suddenly were no longer the special possessions of schools and colleges, no longer the responsibilities of mere ladies and gentlemen. The arts could be had for a membership in lecture societies, a symphony society, or by-the-month clubs purveying music, painting, and literature. Certain bargain-counter programs that prescribe the arts in minimal doses have managed to take root in school curriculums and college programs for the bachelor's degree.

By such false pursuits of easy popularity, certain humanists have admitted false standards and encouraged false expectations. A society that once seriously valued grace in expression, understanding in the arts, and wisdom in worldly affairs was brought to put a higher and higher value on practical information and ready skills legitimately demanded by an economy alternately threatened by the embarrassments of overprosperity and the inroads of depression or war. To expect younger members of this society to preserve the integrity of the humanities was to expect a great deal. We have expected just that, and amazingly often the expectation has been fulfilled.

To expect schools and colleges, their administrations, and their faculties to refuse admission to cultural bargains was to expect even more. In honest attempts to defend the humanities against circumstances of a new age and to meet the cultural need of a new society, we have sometimes surrendered to three processes that have done only disservice to education and to our students.

The first of these processes is that of academic contraction, based upon the inclination to get security, dignity, and integrity by learning more and more about less and less. In some schools this kind of thing has been confused with "discipline"—*disciplina gratia disciplina*. In some colleges it has been confused with scholarly specialization. It should have been confused with neither. Yet many humanists have surrendered their discipline to an outrageous tyranny of mere trivia or have dedicated themselves to mere method—research method, teaching method, critical method.

The second harmful process has stemmed from a devotion to false oracles and false prophets. The compulsion to discover average opinion and to crown that opinion with authority is one result of this practice. Another is the insistence that there must be something oracular about any pronouncement colorfully expressed and widely quoted.

The third process to which we have abandoned too much of humanistic education at all levels is the timid, prudential, pseudo-cultural response to the arts. In a desire to act upon the natural human capacities for sheer enjoyment, or perhaps in a higher-minded encouragement of the natural human impulse to praise beauty and goodness, the humanities have compromised too often with the teaching of so-called appreciation. While "appreciation" had a meaning for an earlier day, in too many quarters it has now become the organized practice of critical insincerity.

The effect of our compromises upon students was inevitable. For the most honest there was strong temptation to dogged revolt. "I hate poetry" has been the flat classroom conclusion of more than one youngster confined by methods of instruction, while outside class, and without any sense of the irony of the situation, he went on writing his own ill-formed verses. His contemporary with less rebellious standards of conduct and a cannier sense of student-teacher tension was led to profess interests he did not feel, to repeat propositions he did not understand, and to echo opinions he did not hold.

In our attempts to meet these youthful indispositions toward formal instructions in the arts we have sometimes succumbed to the wrong sorts of inducements. We have forgotten that to encourage students to set high value on things merely because they are old produces only a false antiquarianism. Now and then we have forgotten, on the other hand, that to encourage students to devote themselves to arts simply because they are currently fashionable is more damaging in academic programs than in popular publications, public theaters, or lecture and concert halls. In these contexts we can get rid of fashions and forget them in a hurry. The classroom, alas, too often makes fashion into a doctrine, then establishes a curriculum upon it. Established there, such doctrines are not innocent embodiments, like fossils in rock; they are degenerative influences, rotten boards, or weak girders in the academic structure.

Antidotes to such weakness are simple but difficult to take. Intellectual honesty, alertness to reality, insistence on values, willingness to judge strictly, competence to judge wisely, and an addiction to excellence—these are the qualities needed to rid the arts of false authority, frills, and hypocrisy.

So much for mistakes and the need of confronting them openly. As for confession of faith, it cannot rely alone on heartening prospects or be supported solely by resolutions of curriculum committees. It must be made inseparable from the daily occupation of the teacher.

Surrendering our natural inclination to play it academically safe, we must tend, as humanists before us tended carefully, the flowers of error. We must reestablish what the scientific disciplines have regularly maintained, the uses of the negative result. We must insist that it is the individual student's right to make his own mistakes, one of the last remaining freedoms of the civilized mind.

With minds hospitable to new ideas, we must recognize that the humanities have a special responsibility to bring into future education a juster sense of time. In a subtler sense than the technical and professional disciplines, the humanities must consider the present in relation to the past. In a way denied to all the arts of certitude, the humanities must be ready, when called upon, to attempt prophecy for the future and to attempt its shaping.

Alertness to time in the educational scheme of things will not make us less keenly aware of immediate opportunities for particulars. We must take advantage of the wonders that science and technology have opened up to humanistic teaching: the great exactness and profusion of record, new mechanics of sight and sound. In other words, we should participate in these changes and not simply applaud them.

Inevitably, then, we will be led to consider the interrelationship of humanistic subjects with other subjects, including the sciences. We must not devote our efforts merely to the humanities, or to education alone, or to teaching simply as a process. We must combine these in the principle that in some respects the most important humanistic education must begin where students leave off their school or college education. To the humanities this observation is more justly applicable than it is to the sciences, to vocational, technical, and professional fields.

In an age of earnest groupism, human experience must still vary. For the uncertain arts in life, individuals are fused differently. We do not know when humanistic education will "go off" in the life of an individual. Our greatest opportunity therefore will come from our greatest handicap. Manifestly we sometimes work with the values of useless knowledge and we should cease our apologies for this fact. Experience that is useless in economic competition is often most rewarding in individual development.

We must confront frankly the importance of inner education. In this phase of education there are often no grades; there are many wordless seminars for which students do not register. We must assume that somewhere in our scheme there is a place, not measured and calculated, for the pleasures of the mind, for the instruction of the heart, for the foundation of ideals, for the reformation of manners, for the lifting of human sights, and for the cultivation of understanding among men—all men.

It will not be the task of the future teachers of the arts of uncertainty to establish airways to Mars, Neptune, and Venus. They will have instead the much harder task of establishing the individual student, fast aging into citizenship, upon foundations proper to himself. Only by that establishment can this future student meet the requirements of those gods with the green eyes who destroy men and women who refuse to live up to mankind's best capabilities. Only by such means will the student make sense in endless time—or in his short, short life.

News and Truth

Texas Quarterly, Summer 1963

M AN is a questioning animal. Two of his pro-
foundest impulses are expressed in the inquiries "What's new?"
and "What's true?" Even for the isolated, the untraveled, the un-
learned, "news" has been made instantaneous and wonderfully
varied. Naturally, therefore, we exaggerate novelty, sensation,
and instant impact.

Since the establishment of the newsbook in the seventeenth century, technology has cut the time of transmission of words and
pictures from months to seconds. Hence the inevitable emphasis
in our time upon the "news beat," the "scoop," the "exclusive."
Hence the tremendous impact of bulletins, true or false, about
national and international events: the ending of World War I
(announced before it happened) and the election of Dewey to the
presidency (which did not happen). Hence the possibility of mis-
taking fiction for fact, as in the case of Orson Welles' personal
invasion of the United States from Mars. Hence the more recent
concern about "managed" news.

All these special circumstances, different as they are, reflect the
same basic condition in the communication system. Time is no
longer required for exchange of information; therefore, time is
often not available for reflection when information most requires
it. In its limited and momentary sense, news as information can
be false and in the baldest sense it can be "managed." But truth
cannot. That distinction should concern everybody involved in
the process—the reader, the publisher, the editor, the reporter.

Keeping ourselves "up-to-date" and "in-the-know" requires a clear view ahead. It also requires an occasional glance backward and time to look around. The fact that what we now call "news" was once called "intelligence" is more than an accident of English vocabulary.

Using that old context for "news" and remembering familiar combinations like "newswriter" and "newsreader," we should arrive at a process of communication that our society obviously needs desperately: "newsthinking." In that process both the relationship between news and truth and the concern of "mass media" about truth and news would be as workable as they are necessary.

It is a good deal easier to write the history of news than it is to write the history of truth. But whoever writes momentary history or makes it by reporting and publishing news had better remember that he must deal ultimately with truth and with history in its longer perspective. Otherwise, the press achieves only a daily intricate splattering of ink, radio and television a succession of noises and illustrated noises, and all of them together a highly temporary circulation of facts as inconsequential as they are transient.

The dailiness of our knowledge therefore cannot relieve us of the responsibility of joining it to the timelessness of mankind's experience. A murder, however sensational and sordid, is death. Under whatever shortened words a headline writer or a commentator chooses to cram it, death is still a part of the universal human lot. Ennoble it or debase it, sensationalize it or sentimentalize it, change its cause or its condition, the truth about it stands.

I knew a publisher once who called his paper's twenty-four–hour grist "a daily diet of mankind's damned foolishness." He took a positive pleasure in setting up and then melting down trivial incident, bright and black prospect, tragedy, whimsy, want ad, jest. It took me almost two years to discover how sensitive this man was to life that kept happening in his town (it was a town, not a city). And how hot the pot in his back shop had to get before it finally burned and bubbled away mere happenings of the day before.

This man was an Englishman. He had the Dickensian name of

T. R. Trubshaw. He was uneasy in the day of comic strip and announcer, columnist and canned editorial. He would have felt better—and he might have done better—in the days when Addison and Steele shot their lace cuffs and dipped quills into man's foibles and coffeehouse talk and philosophic ascensions. Actually, though, he lived in a little town in North Dakota. He published a little daily called the *Times-Record*. He paid his bills by printing dismal and interminable "legals." But, like Socrates, he somehow succeeded in bringing philosophy from heaven down to earth.

Trubshaw had the courage of his main conviction. That conviction was that plain ignorance is a healthier state than false persuasion and that nothing wears worse than a secondhand opinion or a fashionable falsehood.

Trubshaw is dead. I am not sure, but I suspect that he died of apoplexy. I saw him almost die of apoplexy many times, including the night he ran his foreman out of the shop for printing a boiler-plate editorial on the beauties of Niagara Falls in the midst of a terrible Dakota drought.

Mere respect for fact will do a lot for a news "medium." It will, among other things, keep it out of libel suits and, if the facts are interesting or significant, out of bankruptcy. But that is only the first step. Much more difficult is the responsibility imposed by loyalty to truth, arrived at by trial and innumerable errors. That responsibility is inescapable in publishing that serves a community, because the community of a newspaper is not separate, but inseparable, from mankind.

Hence the local preoccupation of journalism must always be news; but its wider profession should always be truth. The main problems in this communication of truth are not the obvious but the subtle pitfalls in exchange of ideas. The tyranny of words is quite as dangerous as the tyranny of man. Perversion of ways of talking common sense and spreading current news will just as surely undermine a nation's ability to sort out beliefs and purposes as armed rebellion or violent dictatorship. Your Hitlers, Mussolinis, Khrushchevs, and Castros know this. They know too that, if people can be got to dwell solely on perverse or trivial issues,

energy first can be drained from popular discussion and mass devotion then can be diverted to any kind of purpose.

If news media are to grow in significance, they will have to
convince a new generation of truth-seekers that there is no reward
greater than the enlarging experience, the zest for getting news
written and getting the truth of the news to readers and listeners.

With full recognition of the importance of economic, social, and
political problems that beset topmost levels of journalism, we
should pay more attention to the two more numerous groups who
maintain the foundation of the whole process, the reporter and
his public, and their common concern.

Confronted with the modern news organizations, too few very
young and very ambitious students set their sights on the most
important role in what, alas, we have been compelled to call the
"communication arts." I mean the role of the reporter. In the
sense in which I use the word, reporters often turn up wearing
other organizational titles: bureau chief, war correspondent,
stringer, free-lance writer. But in essence they are reporters still
—reporters first, last, and essentially.

All of us who have been in and out of news shops remember
such men. I wish now to recall only three. The first was an Irishman who spent all his working days with a large news-gathering
organization. He won his share of honors and plaudits, sat in
awesome offices, and was finally called upon to form and imple-
ment high policy. But he never quit being a reporter. From the
eminence of the skilled reporter he constantly interpreted the process of getting and writing news to newly hired newspapermen.
He broke in reporters on facts. Truth and the historical interpretation of truth followed. But first, the facts.

To one reporter, full of words and nighttime energy, he gave a
stern and memorable lesson in this essential. He had allowed two
paragraphs for the murder of an unknown citizen. The beginner
(beginners were never called "cubs" in that organization) gave
the first paragraph to the fact that William Smith had been killed
at midnight, etc. The "etc." flowered in the second paragraph to
a vivid circumstantial account.

It took two hours of listening to the Irishman's blistering comments for the beginner to learn that the murdered man was not, according to the official record, William Smith but William Johnson Smith, Jr. (one of numerous William Smiths) and the murder had taken place at 12:07, which was not midnight of one day but early morning of the next. Corrected, the story was one paragraph of accurate fact; the vividly reported second paragraph was killed.

Still a beginner, that reporter went on to other work. As he left, Brian Bell sent him a note in very black pencil on newsprint. It was not about facts. It said: "I hope you look back often to what you found in reporting. I hope that when you walk the daylight street, you will keep the sense of aliveness you may have learned in this midnight room. I suspect that sometimes when nothing is happening to you, you will recall the men here, keeping tab for you on what is happening and what these events mean."

The second reporter, in one of his last assignments, was a war correspondent whose uncannily accurate statistics on tanks in the African campaign became a major source of military intelligence. Invalided by his paper to Latin America, his last report—early in 1945—was not statistical. It concluded: "The war that is now being fought to unconditional surrender will have won nothing—indeed, it will have lost everything—if the people of all the Americas (Cuba in little and Argentina in large) are not won to the common enterprise of freedom, not of parliaments only, but also of individual men." John Whitaker's adding-machine mind could spell out interpretation as well as subtract and divide figures.

The third reporter never moved from a midwestern paper that gave him a job during the Great Depression. Toward the end of that job, in a neglected account of his young experience that deserved more readers, F. Hopkinson Smith made sense of the kind of experience from which his famous forebear had been able to achieve only a literary reputation: "Working on this newspaper has taught me a new word—'sympathy.' I used to think it was a sentimental term for gushing. Now I see it may mean a talent for entering into the lives of other people, and understanding our own lives better for that experience."

All three men had seen and had practiced the principle that there is a connection between news and truth more than historical, sentimental, or journalistic; it is the link between man's understanding of his present life and his conviction about the significance of living.

It is this sense of significance which the real reporter provides the reader, no matter what that reader's state of mind or condition of life. At the reporter's fingertips, the multiple fact becomes the single report and the single report may become the thinking material of the multiple minds of his readers. It is as if the reporter were at the centerpoint of the double funnel by which "intelligence," in the seventeenth-century sense, still pours in and then pours out again. This is not a comfortable or merely routine position. It is a point of intense and wide responsibility.

At that essential point, news media need—because their readers and listeners and lookers need—all the mind, sense, and wisdom journalism schools can possibly produce, all the talent and devotion a long tradition can possibly encourage.

The Educations of a Doctor

Dallas Medical Journal, October 1960

WITH the possible exception of football coaches on Monday morning, doctors get more daily unsolicited opinion about their work than do members of any other profession. Somehow every citizen shares in the deep-running tribal myth that, given other circumstances, he would have made a great surgeon, a quarterback, or a psychiatrist. The time has come for the medical profession to demand credentials from those of us who pontificate about medicine and medical education.

Like most comments on the lifework that an M.D. undertakes, mine sprout from nostalgic and casual experience and a deep unsupported belief that, although much is still wrong with humanity, medical sciences can help make some of it intelligible even when nobody can set any of it right.

My first acquaintance with medicine was highly anecdotal. It came from family stories about medical forebears who had left their immediate descendants very little to live on but a great deal to talk about. None of this talk would have offended Hippocrates, none of it was scientific, not much was heroic; but the sum made a small boy want to be a doctor when he grew up.

I grew up in a fifty-bed hospital. I owe that upbringing to a near relative, a gallant lady who many years before had left a mid-Victorian female seminary to enter upon medical-missionary training. In those earlier generations such training, you will recall, consisted of unequal doses of *materia medica*, Gray's *Anatomy*, and the Old Testament prophets. Advantage clearly lay with Old

Testament prophecy, which somehow accented and directed rather than diverted or subdued that lady's passion for the arts of healing. Accordingly, from the age of nine to nineteen, off and on, my home was a small room in a wonderfully disorganized establishment that served the uncertain medical needs of a college and adjoining mountain communities of miners, bootleggers, farmers, and summer visitors. The polite seasonal ailments of the summer visitors added a touch of something like gaiety to what otherwise probably would have been a very solemn environment for a boy.

From this vantage point, in a kind of triangulation among the morgue in the basement, obstetrical rooms on the top floor, and a jumble of humanity at the entrance—now called the out-patient clinic—I watched doctors, usually at work. I watched one doctor in particular. He died of the practice of his profession more than a quarter of a century ago. These facts date and more or less define the origin of my title and the basis of my comments here.

The educations of a doctor are plural in many ways. For one thing, each patient, no matter how manifest his ailment or how routine his cure, renews in the doctor's experiences his education for medicine, about which his M.D. is only one overt sign.

A good deal of sense and nonsense has been pronounced about the personal relationships in which a doctor engages. From general superficialities, usually described by such labels as "bedside manner," to the unmastered and unimagined calculus of individualities in human suffering, the doctor faces problems of human being more directly than any other person.

For the lawyer and his client, for the scientist and his disciple, for the religious leader and his follower, there is always a distinct third being or a removed third body of knowledge, custom, and belief that dominates the relation. The law itself, scientific principle itself, ultimate objects of religion themselves stay in the ascendant above the two and may keep intervening between them. For legal justice and abstract knowledge and religious credo— profound or not, personalized or impersonal, perfect or perverted —will always inform and govern what goes on between A and B (in lawyer's office and court, in laboratory and lecture room, at the altar and in the confessional). But the doctor and his patient do not set up their rest and cannot work out their relationship for the mere sake of effecting medical cure, nor can they bow to the mere advancement of medical science—unless, that is, the patient is already a cadaver.

An important corollary to this point is that the roles of lawyer, scientist, and religious worker may occasionally be threaded into the practice of medicine. At successive points in his living and practice the doctor may well be governed exclusively by one or another of these unmedical considerations. Nothing is so intimate about disease or so private about any medical practice as to exclude the social implications when the disease has reached epidemic proportions or when the practice runs counter to the legal and social responsibilities to protect a group. Similarly, times come when natural laws, as immutable as those professed by physicist or chemist, must take over and the patient lie down and the doctor leave the room. Nor is it necessary for patient and doctor to take their relationship into a sanctuary to discover that there are moments in human existence when miracle drug and miraculous electronic probe and miracle-working surgeon's fingers are less significant than cause and effect that, for want of a better term, we are left to call "spiritual."

These are more than polite concessions of the obvious. The doctor shares with lawyer, with scientist, with minister, rabbi, and priest many obvious social, physical, and spiritual attributes. These serve only to return us to the main predication about a doctor: every new patient is a new bringing forth, a new education for him. This would still be true though his own medical practice were limited to one disease of one organ curable by only one prescription.

Admitting the dangers of mere antiquarianism in any science such as medicine, I would suggest that doctors revive the tricorn and tricolor modes of the Middle Ages. By very general description, then, their perspectives would be triple: external, internal, eternal.

Among the external and newly essential perspectives for new

M.D.s are all the not-patient, not-human factors: the chemistries, the environments, the economies, and the ecologies of medicine. These will change in time. Medicine has a vastly outward-expanding relevance to faraway influences and perplexities as panoramic as the physical effects of cosmic rays and as utopian as the systems for keeping man alive in outer space. Closer in are medicine's external scientific relationships among the burgeoning discoveries in nuclear physics, biochemistry, and a whole panoply of microsciences.

These are the landscapes of medicine. No doctor can now expect to be merely altruistic about the state of public health or merely folksy in doing good. By no such means can he find his way among the changing and brand-new avenues of his profession.

Quite as complex are internal perspectives. The inward searching of medicine is symbolic as well as physical, though the merely physical design is complex enough. In the seventeenth century physicians in the Royal Society were configuring man as a wonderful kind of microcosm. Today they would have better reason to do so. Bodies of knowledge like cytology and new instruments of observation like the electron microscope have made a stellar constellation not of man's whole body but of any cubic centimeter of his flesh and blood.

But these wonders are primary and these manifestos are primer stuff compared with the uncharted savannahs of feeling with which the doctor must cope. A Texas doctor who took his M.D. more than a century ago put the whole intimacy and the whole vastness into one sentence in 1870. Writing in his journal in Victoria he confessed: "I have had terrifying occasion to pause before I visited upon a fellow man some simple medicament and have known a constant surge of uncertainty before I used a blade on a human being. But this perplexity is nothing compared with the simple difficulty of talking with a child about his pain or telling even a very old man that now the time has come for him to die."

By whatever scientific or intellectual device doctors put forward these external and internal views, they cannot escape the still wider principle that their practice is limitless and eternal in its relations. Modern medicine is inextricably a part of continuing tradition, a tradition expressed in only one way by the Hippocratic oath.

In medical schools today no textbook, lecture, or laboratory preparation confronts wholly the spirit of health and the dispirit and exaltation of illness and death. These have been communicated by people young doctors have known, especially by doctors they have known in medical schools.

In a more literal sense than any other kind of university graduate, M.D.s must expand curriculum in practice and in belief. How and with what must they identify themselves, where lend themselves, where give themselves, where withhold themselves? They must undertake a long series of canny and courageous assaults upon ill-being. Much of their vision must be intuitive, for not even very modern doctors wear electron microscopes in their coat pockets.

It is neither comfort nor discouragement that, unlike the work of other professions, every single thing doctors do is temporary. For every cure, like all good physical health, is still subject to ultimate defeat. Man is still mortal. That fact is not the despair of science but its limitless challenge.

In this sense, medical education must draw upon all that the doctor has seen and learned and imagined in the years of his formal learning. The company of his fellows, the traditions that have sustained centuries of medicine, and the promises that medicine now makes to society are as important as the inventions his generation will welcome. The inventions will change things and will change themselves. But essential human qualities stand fast. As the Victorian doctor wrote in his 1870 journal, "The doctor walks with these, or there is no going."

The Collection of Knowledge in Texas

Texas Quarterly, Winter 1958*

THE underpinnings of this discussion are certain assumptions or beliefs that must be stated bluntly at the start:

— that it is the duty of any cultural entity like Texas to keep its intellectual purposes clear and to keep up with its intellectual obligations;

— that the essential tradition of Texas is based upon human values easy to recognize and hard to realize;

— that Texans today, recognizing these values, stand ready to maintain them realistically;

— that Texas, which now ranks high in private income among all the other states within the Union, has the material power to fulfill its intellectual obligations in practical ways.

For these reasons I propose that there be established somewhere in Texas—let's say in the capital city—a center of cultural compass, a research center to be the Bibliothèque Nationale of the only state that started out as an independent nation.

The main business of the first "learned society" in Texas was originally described as "the collection and diffusion of knowledge." The society's earliest memorial puts its program of action in these terms: "Texas having fought the battles of liberty . . . now thrown upon her internal resources for the permanence of her

* Previously printed by Carl Hertzog as a brochure for the Philosophical Society of Texas, 1957.

institutions, moral and political, calls upon all persons to use all their efforts for the increase and diffusion of knowledge and sound information."

Collection of knowledge, considered as a social responsibility of the state—and that is how the Philosophical Society in 1837 did consider it—is a complex process. I intend to treat a single phase of the process and to treat that phase simply.

Whenever groups of men—societies, political associations, states, and nations—have set about to keep their minds alive and ready to meet the future, they have paid some attention to history. Before the proposal of a focal point of our intellectual resources, a brief prologue, more or less historical, is proper.

Knowledge can be collected in many ways, the most obvious of which is the collection of knowledgeable people. Our learned teaching faculties and our inventive research staffs do not represent better collecting of this kind than did the assets of certain ancient kingdoms. A lively trade in minds was partly responsible for classical and medieval wisdom. When seers were not indigenous, they were often imported. Some were lured to a metropolis because it had a reputation for cherishing knowledge; some were literally kidnapped; some were brought to court by worldly blandishments that make industry's recent raids on college faculties look puny and penny minded. Many an emperor accomplished more (and, indeed, attained a more nearly permanent glory) by capturing wise men than by winning battles; more by cultivating philosophers than by cutting down political enemies. But trade in living minds, scholars on the hoof, could not suffice for the development of Western civilization.

It is an obvious law of nature that collections of living men, however wise, constitute highly perishable collections of knowledge. Enlightened human minds almost invariably outmode themselves by encouraging continual search for new knowledge, new synthesis. Furthermore, no matter how great their undertaking or how vast their accomplishment, all knowing men are sooner or later overtaken by death. So the collection of permanent records has always been essential to civilization.

In looking far backward one is tempted to speculate upon the motives that originally brought men to collect the tokens of man's experience, imagination, discovery, and calculation. Can the drive that brought on Europe's periodic seasons of vast intellectual hunger be explained by grand maxims like Knowledge Is Power? Should it be interpreted more idealistically: collection of knowledge has always enlarged perspective, allowing men to see a little past the borders of their own experience? Or must the impulse be reduced to something just above the motives of the packrat: collection helps collectors to endure life's inescapable moments of insecurity? No matter what the explanation, it was long ago that men determined to save man's records from oblivion. Whatever gave it force, that determination shaped our intellectual history. It still shapes our intellectual history.

To the unwitting the process of getting knowledge together appears at times either lumbering or ludicrous. Yet unexpected increments have kept coming from apparently "useless" collections of knowledge; odd conglomerations of things or facts or ideas have often brought about profound public benefit or done historic service to the common weal. For example, a case of Pacific-island birds' eggs contributed to the strategy of a great military campaign. Trays of ancient coins were used to revise our knowledge of ancient political chronology. In the nineteenth century a museum of human brains gave impetus to that wing of mental philosophy known today as experimental psychology. A collection of fossils provided new light for the assumptions of anthropology. Rare stamp albums are still the source of essential information about engraving methods. There was a time when a series of oil well cores would have been considered a useless geological gatherum; yet the first extensive collection of such chunks of the lower world did great service to the oil industry, and later collections still serve it.

Admittedly, some collecting looks foolish and may be so in fact. Only morbid curiosity seems to justify the preservation anywhere —much less in Austin, Texas—of miscellaneous locks of hair from the heads of statesmen like Napoleon and poets like Shelley. But memory of what even stranger collections than this have wrought in the past will make one hesitate to predict that this haircut museum will never, never contribute to learning.

Of all systematic collections of knowledge, those called libraries are most easily explained. An agreeable if uncertain chapter in this history is the account of the making of the library at Alexandria. Here is a paraphrase of one version of it taken from Parsons' *Alexandrian Library* (p. 418):

When Ptolemy Philadelphius, one of the Kings of Alexandria, ruled, he attracted to himself knowledge and learned men. And he searched for books of wisdom and gave orders to have them brought to him. And he set apart for them libraries where they were to be collected. And he put in charge of them a man called Zumayra, the son of Murra, who was zealous in their collection and procurement, and Zumayra paid high prices for the provision of them. He asked Zumayra, saying, "Do you suppose there are other books of wisdom on this earth which we do not have?" And Zumayra told him: "There are some books in China, India, Persia, ...Babylon, and also among the Romans that we do not have." And the King was pleased, and told him to keep on collecting.

When that library in Alexandria went up in smoke, man's zeal for bringing together the record of human experience did not evaporate. In Rome, in Paris, in improbable places from Ireland to obscure Oriental palaces, the zeal for preservation of knowledge asserted itself. Sometimes this zeal also spent itself. But in whatever places or at whatever time it died out, that dying out was never the end of it.

Some historians err in assuming that this urge to collect the human record has been implemented only by well-organized societies, by sophisticated national or local groups with the high gloss of long cultivation. As a matter of fact, one is tempted to say that wherever there was a frontier in America there was a counterfrontier and that the main purpose of this counterfrontier was not only to help man grow or dig or catch or kill his living but also to put this man in communication with the traditions of his kind and thereby secure to his descendants the benefits of the free mind.

Through the Constitution this counterfrontier spirit guaranteed the right of intellectual creation. It was this spirit that founded in Philadelphia a Philosophical Society that is still busy with the advancement of knowledge. It was this counterfrontier spirit that conceived the Library of Congress in terms bigger than the legislator's need to look up legal authorities. It was this spirit in the Philosophical Society of Texas that caused to be appointed among the society's first officers a librarian.

Although, to be effective, great collections of knowledge have always required public support and although most great collections have pursued a policy of wide public benefit, the growing points of such intellectual enterprise have often been stimulated by individual collectors, purchasers, or donors. By such private intellectual enterprise, public imagination is fired; without it, public interest burns low.

To this principle of the relation of public interest to private exploit in collecting must be added an American corollary: in the United States, many of the great movers of intellectual material have been men of practical affairs. Henry Huntington, as the powerful investor in American railroads, developed a huge realism about business and society before the Huntington Library became a reality. His greatness lay in the sweep of his operations. Few men in the history of amassing knowledge, before or since, have matched his enormous strides. Yet his formula was as simple as the combination of railroad interests: he collected collections.

Henry Clay Folger, whose perspective was different but whose final accomplishments were equally great, first attained eminence in the petroleum industry (he was chairman of the board of Standard Oil). His vision was specific but not narrow; he dreamed the complete collection of Shakespeare, not only of the words but also of every conceivable subject Shakespearean—the life, times, sources, stage history, and criticism. It is an interesting commentary on the permeative qualities of collected knowledge that today the library in Washington that bears Folger's name is a center for the study of early American civilization. (Not even the wildest zealots who live on theories that Shakespeare did not write Shakespeare have yet suggested that Shakespeare was an American.)

From 1837 to 1856, the *scriptorium*, the *biblioteca* of Western tradition that had become well established in our culture was transported to Texas. In examining the tradition our Texas predecessors had bifocal vision, historic and prophetic. They looked backward to the great accumulations of knowledge like the Alexandrian Library; they also looked forward to the future needs of Texas. Something of what they saw and what we owe to their longsightedness should be recalled.

Early Texans were highly informal about such undertakings. Let us not for that reason underestimate the mere accomplishments in Texas before 1900 or discount their social and economic influence on the development of this state. The first Texas lawmakers, lacking a Library of Congress, borrowed their books in great numbers from an Austin merchant who had invested in cotton and the classics. The historical significance of this fact has been obscured by such quaint reports as the one that this Austin merchant bought two dozen egg baskets in which to deliver books to the lawmakers. There is a steady testimony in the eighteenthirties, -forties, and -fifties that Texas professional men, especially lawyers, doctors, businessmen, and theologians, insisted that Texas must have collections of knowledge available for immediate recourse and for future development. Of course collections of knowledge have always had their detractors. Texas has produced her share of such detractors, some in official positions. In every generation, "Act, don't think" has been the special plea of people who are afraid of the works of the mind. Two years after the Philosophical Society was founded in Texas, the *Houston Morning Star* entered such a plea:

WE WANT NO MORE MEN OF
TALENT IN TEXAS

Heaven knows that one of the greatest obstacles to the advancement of her interests has ever been the overwhelming number of men of talent. We want no more lawyers, physicians, or ministers for the next 20 years.

Despite such understandable preoccupation with short-range tasks of a developing economy, Texas has accomplished a good deal since the date of that complaint and since the days when legislators borrowed their books in egg baskets from a general store on Congress Avenue.

At the turn of the century the vice-consul from Norway and Sweden, who kept that store, gave to the people of Texas the first research library in the state. Somewhat later an institute dedicated partly to the advancement of science arranged to import from Europe what, until recently, was the largest single collection of learned serials in this part of the world. By painfully slow stages a professor in a church-supported college built a research library upon the name of a single writer. Canny investment of an early endowment helped to develop a small city library on the coast into a productive center for study. Here and there other local establishments—under the aegis of a college, church, regional museum, or small archives—made independent contributions. To name every such independent development would require a long page indeed. In connection with these collections of knowledge, public and private, it should be remembered that many of them have been occupied with the simple problem of keeping open. The state owes a great debt to the donors, trustees, and librarians who have managed that difficult task.

Between World War I and the Great Depression three major research collections came together in Texas. The first was bought for Texans by a cattleman and banker from the heirs of a Chicago broker. It was a magnificent library, partly because the principal agent in its collection had been that redoubtable bibliographer and famous dealer in rare aromatic oils, Thomas J. Wise. Texans felt some embarrassment and some consternation when it was discovered that this same Wise also had been the most prolific book forger of all time. A happy ending—and somehow happy endings are appropriate to this kind of story—came in the slow realization that, precisely because Wise the forger had built the library, Texas possessed an almost unparalleled collection of remarkable books that for purposes of research were quite as important as the hypothetical first editions might have been.

Soon another collection joined the first. It was more pedestrian in origin, getting its start with the books of an amateur scholar who made his living in the British postal service. When this man died, his library was offered for sale. There is nothing memorable about the story up to this point. But the collection was purchased by act of the Texas Legislature. Many state legislatures since that time have followed the example set in Texas. Texas has too seldom repeated it.

The third collection to become part of the state's resources was founded by a Texas housewife upon a simple family library and was extended by her, with the help of wide-roaming agents, into an important source of knowledge. Few libraries of any kind have been more natural in their origin, few have worked more immediate good, and very few of the same size have spread their influence more widely.

Later annals of this kind of collection in Texas continued to be lively. A noteworthy experiment in Dallas has suggested the uses of photography in gathering knowledge; a Texas battle monument has become an important scholarly center. Revived interest in local archives throughout the state preceded the recent clamor about the major public collections in the capital city. A newspaper foundation has brought to Texas a great literary collection. A businessman and a building associate have joined their philanthropies in fortifying a new collection. A geologist and bookman, by gift of his private library of modern writing, has led a talented company of young scholars into new fields of study. All this is venture capital placed upon the sound business proposition that Texas has an intellectual future.

Yet, against these gains, we count our losses. For example, a major collection of Americana specially suited to research in Texas was recently offered to the state. It went to California. The result of another lapse is that New Haven, Connecticut, not Austin, must hereafter be the place where scholars study two out of three of the rare sources of Texas history before 1845. It is a pleasure, of course, to think of a Texas center in a great private university in the East. Certainly Texas should be studied more (and also more seriously, if one is to judge by reports of the state in current magazines and reflections of it in recent cinema). On the other hand, it is disturbing to note that, simply because for many years Texans have had their hands full, instruments of learning have slipped past.

To questions about guaranteeing the intellectual future of Texas there is no single answer. But from the books of the first Philosophical Society, we can take at least one leaf: that which pleads for the collection of knowledge. Why should Texas not establish in the capital city, in connection with the state university and in affiliation with all the related libraries owned by the people of Texas, a center for such collection, a "central" for the diffusion of information? The great urban, regional, and national centers for the collection of knowledge in London, Paris, Dublin, and Edinburgh were begun on an almost pitiable fraction of what this state could spend. A library research center would save its operating expenses in moneys now spent by Texas institutions, industries, and individuals who must either go where knowledge has been massively collected or do without.

Future Texans will be too ambitious to do without. What is more important than comparisons of expense with savings is the fact that by means of such a research center Texas could attract more of the talent, skill, knowledge, and wisdom that it needs now and will need in the future. We can now afford expenditure of Texas moneys. We cannot afford the waste or the loss of Texas minds.

Texas has accomplished much. It still has much more to accomplish. If those who believe profoundly that the state has not reached the top of its intellectual bent are accused by their contemporaries of making disloyal sounds, they may appeal to the proclamation made in 1837 by certain newcomers, including Mirabeau Lamar, Ashbel Smith, and Sam Houston: "Texas calls on her intelligent and patriotic citizens to furnish to the rising generation the means of instruction within our own borders." This was no mere summons to meet the immediate, practical needs of a new republic. These men were capable of looking into the future, and what they saw is still a major responsibility.

The argument goes full circle and returns to the ancient need of every knowing society: the collection of knowledgeable people. By the development of a center comparable to the great national and regional libraries, each of which began with more modest foundations than Texas has already laid, the state would get to itself more than past glories, more than tremendous uses of the permanent records of man's attainments. It would get here, develop here, and keep here more creative minds, the first essential in the collection and diffusion of knowledge.

The Public Library
and Private Welfare

Address, Friends of Texas Libraries, Austin, 1958*

I N America the inner standards of our living are best symbolized and best sustained by public libraries. Numerous writers have recorded the ideals and accomplishments, the handicaps and feats of public collections of books. From a quick reference to the card catalogue, I gather that a hundred or more authors, at least, have sung general praises, and literally innumerable devotees have hymned specific collections. The great ancient gatherings of books, brought together by canny if not wise monarchs and re-created by learned slaves, monastic scriptoriums and the manuscripts they established or scattered, old books bound by chains to their little circles to discourage bookish thieves—all these make good stories, good illustrations for popular volumes. In no such book does it become apparent, however, that collections of this sort have worked their way into the center of what man believes about himself and about much else. In no volume that I have found is there any real assessment of the effect of public libraries on man's major social concerns or his major community purposes.

If we begin with what we can trace closely, we will choose to start, perhaps, with the mechanics libraries of the eighteenth century or those vague and profitable ventures into circulating libraries by pre-French-revolutionary booksellers. If we seek a single place of departure, we may ignore all this earlier development

* Published in another version by *Texas Libraries*, 1959.

and hurry down the years to a later point when we can set up our argument in the great Reading Room of the British Museum. Within such walls Europe and Western civilization got their most seminal ideas, even more than in the palaces that housed great consults, political meetings that were said to divide the world, and even more than in the vast museums that inspired a new great art. Some ideas were re-creations of the past by men like Gibbon and Carlyle; some were new systems like Mill's; some were assaults upon the future, like the tawdry but terrible sentences that Karl Marx wrote in a London library room marked FOR READERS ONLY.

In this country symbols and attainments of reality behind the symbols are less complex. Too many people think they are so simple that if one has enough money he can go out and buy them. To the public, conscious of public buildings, a "Carnegie library" meant for two generations a structure that housed a town's main store of written things. In places as different as Boston, Charleston, New York, and Charlottesville, the library that was semi-public (like the Athenaeum or the walls that Thomas Jefferson designed and that still enclose Virginia's best books) had a more selective influence. On a grander and more completely public scale the New York Public Library—a cluster of foundations, a big dim building guarded by big blank-eyed lions—became a university of the people, a congregation of learning for many minds, many tongues, all social levels, all points of view. Undoubtedly, some new Marx—or perhaps some new St. John—has already, within the knowledgeable caverns of that place, written his manifesto for the future or an Apocalypse for our children's children.

I do not use carelessly that staid and stilted academic term "university" to describe a great public library. I mean the public library should be an educational institution in more than the nineteenth-century mot: "A university is a collection of books." For the theoretical scientist and the poet, as for the historian and the mechanic designer, such an institution fulfills completely, even down to little obvious points, the definition of "a university."

I would not limit to the "advanced" or "adult" level this identity of the library with public education. If one polled the graduating classes in all American public high schools, he would find in the libraries of their towns and cities an astonishing and quite specific educational influence upon the abler students. Much of the communication between the school student and the public library comes about merely because communities starve their schools with too few books. I would emphasize the extraordinary opportunities that many public libraries have given younger students to come close to a critical mass of books. In such a mass there are benefits that machines have no power to measure.

The inhibitions of organized learning and the unconscious tyrannies of organized teaching often discourage the illumination that comes easily into a natural context where at the bookshelf also stands a baker's wife, a delivery boy, or a retired business-man. It seldom comes vividly at first; it sometimes comes se-cretly; it is often unconscious in the community of worded things that a library—especially a hospitable, completely accessible, and usable public library—best provides.

So far I have kept close to the so-called book. Since it lies at the heart of the work I profess, I am not willing to obscure it or diminish its importance by laying first emphasis upon important newer things with which a library deals. Yet the library does deal in many newer things, and must. There are, for example, pictures. The ability of a library to bring great art to a community through reproductions, however distant and obscure, has long since been demonstrated. There are further unexplored possibilities for co-operation between the public library and the museum and among museums, artists, and libraries for exhibition of art of all sorts. Conversely, great museums of painting and sculpture now present music and also publish or lend books.

Then there are the facts of new library technologies. A great confusion has risen from our failure to acknowledge that photo-graphic reproduction of words is a much greater departure in reading habit than that caused by the invention of movable type and the first publication of printed books. One of the major under-takings of the public library should be the acquainting of young readers—the word customers of the future—with various new, quite wonderful means of reading words photographically recorded, reproduced, projected.

I wish now to ignore the mere historic accomplishment and needs of the public library and to discuss briefly two sorts of investment that bring any community tremendous social, economic, and cultural returns.

The first proposal, barely intimated in some public library systems, is a cooperative record, research, reference, and reading program between business institutions and the public library and among libraries in a particular locality. The principle is easy enough to hit squarely, even if we miss the mark in particulars: in any group in which the individual members—institutional or personal—do not have available a collection sufficient for regular needs, the best way of providing for the need is to establish in a public library a common collection. Many special subjects cannot be collected by schools, hospitals, and other public institutions individually. A cooperative purchase and reference program, located in the public library, would build facilities unobtainable otherwise, at least a generation earlier. Furthermore, every such participation is tax deductible.

Second, to put one good book into circulation among ten minds will buy more social good than any other similar investment. If one thousand people in an area that supports a population of one million would invest the price of two yearly magazine subscriptions in the free moneys of a public library, that sum would revolutionize library service. Such donations should not be for mending roofs, repairing floors, or buying catalogue cards. They should be gambled on the imagination of the librarians to push words out into the imagination of the community.

The public library's progress with new machinery for conveying ideas, its responsibilities to new and vastly enlarged demands of multiple readers, cannot be put off and therefore must not be minimized. Yet the library's greatest mission will always be to single, and single-minded, persons bent on the pursuit of useful information or the enjoyment of casual reading experience. The library, then, must be at once universally concerned with common

good and minutely interested in the individual—and individual-
istic—reader. We need the public library if we are to sustain our
public education and fortify our private welfare, the inner standard of living.

The Collector and Copyright

Address, Collector's Institute, U.T. Arlington, 1974

THESE remarks are not intended either as legal advice or as solemn warning. They are general observations drawn from long-standing interest in the history of literary property and in the collection of books, manuscripts, and graphic arts.

Among the collector's major problems today, copyright is less manifest than inflation of prices, increasing competition in most fields, erroneous but widespread impressions that there is little left to collect, and universal need for restoration and preservation of what has been collected. No collector worthy of his shelves is halted by such problems.

Yet collectors should not be blithely indifferent to any significant condition of their work. The body of law related to literary property has sometimes been dismissed by the cavalier conclusion, "This is a serious matter, but don't bother about it." The sense of my comments is that some of the vital conditions of collecting are involved, and for that reason alone copyright is worth the emphasis first made systematic in the eighteenth century.

In that earlier period, Edmund Curll's more positive qualities —which most eighteenth-century contemporaries thought were not numerous—included a collector's acquisitiveness and an indiscreet printer's aggressiveness. Having obtained unpublished manuscript letters of Alexander Pope, he published his collection in 1741. The resulting suit, Pope versus Curll, established the perpetual right of the author in unpublished manuscript materials and of others legally claiming under the original right. The legal principle was confirmed in 1774 by a common-law decision involving Lord Chesterfield's letters.

The common-law cases on manuscript rights of Pope and Chesterfield were specially significant because the first English copyright statute (1710) had not included a definition of rights in unpublished matter. Apart from the fact that the 1710 statute was the first copyright law, its short title, An Act for the Encouragement of Learning, was prophetic for collectors.

Encouragement of learning by private collection is no mere sentiment. It is long-established fact. Today, of course, the advancement of knowledge is much more complex than it was in 1774. New technologies in this century have vastly increased facilities for making and distributing copies. They also have caused certain difficulties for both institutions and small private libraries. In advancing the spread of knowledge, a collector or curator is enabled by relatively simple and cheap methods of reproduction to share manuscript text. Assuming that a manuscript has been acquired without assignment of copyright deriving from the author, what kind of access to the manuscripts can be legally provided?

At this point the law is often hazy. Exhibition of manuscript or description in a published catalogue, without inclusion of substantial parts of the text, has seldom been challenged. Reproduction and unrestricted distribution of entire manuscripts, even for virtuous purposes, such as help to students or assistance of scholarly publication, are much more risky. [A "public" library located in the United States and owning property rights in an unpublished work may, since January 1, 1978, reproduce a copy or a phonorecord of the unpublished work to protect against loss or destruction of the original and may also reproduce a copy or a phonorecord to distribute to another "public" library for use there by researchers.—Ed.] Publication for profit—institutional or personal—greatly increases the risk. Furthermore, a collector who engages in outright commercial use to the detriment of the copyright owner may subject himself to a higher schedule of damages.

This is a proper point at which to mention certain misconceptions about literary property shared by some collectors and other keepers of manuscripts.

The first is the assumption that semiliterate or illiterate manuscript or printed writing is not subject to law. Among earlier judges, Lord Mansfield made the point that a court is not concerned with judging literary or social merit in protecting authors, their heirs and assigns. Mansfield's opinion still obtains. That opinion reminds collectors that unlettered men and women have made notable contributions to records of life through stories, memoirs, songs, and accounts of incident, custom, and manners.

The second misconception is that manuscript additions to a printed volume, such as notes on blank leaves, interleaved supplements, or marginalia, are not the property of the writer. They are. For various reasons, specially significant to collectors, added matter of this kind can be valuable. Legally, they do not become an integral part of the printed text merely because they are made physically inseparable from a copy of it.

The third misconception is that official printed documents and legal decisions are sacrosanct literary property. Both categories of publication usually lie in the public domain. I would add a totally subjective opinion. Critics, historians, and teachers of English have neglected too long the fact that opinions written by judges like Holmes and Cardozo as well as historic official statements written by, or for, some eminent modern officeholders contain writing worthy of the most discriminating collector.

Samuel Clemens provided perhaps the most ironic example of literary property in the public domain. He was more deeply concerned with copyright than was any other great American author. He took advantage of successive copyright under his own name, Samuel Clemens, and his pen name, Mark Twain; he registered that pen name; and he ended his career with ardent support of the rights of authors. The latter activity brought about a contradiction for collectors. As published in the works first collected, his speech on copyright before Congress is a relatively dull essay. His actual congressional testimony, stenographically transcribed, reads and sounds more like the author, whose tongue was as agile as his pen. Because the more readable version became a public document, it was not copyrighted.

The fact that the first congressional printing of this manuscript is hard to come by is a reminder that not all official documents, usually published at a low price, are still cheap. Vast pulping operations, especially those during the First World War, have made many government publications scarce and correspondingly costly.

To return to specifics concerning collection, I would guess that the most common request made of a collector is for exhibition of pieces from his collection. Exhibition of unpublished materials is a helpful and usually safe procedure. It is safest when less than a complete composition is shown. Responsibility lies mainly on the exhibitor. Sometimes, however, an excess of legal piety may increase burdens. Recently a library, determined to observe copyright meticulously, included in exhibit cases a boldly printed legend: UNPUBLISHED—NOT TO BE COPIED. The curators discovered that this warning stimulated many visitors to write down everything they could see through the glass cases. When the sign was removed, copying ceased. It is not uncommon for collectors and libraries to encounter in addition to specific laws and regulations the unpredictable orneriness of human nature.

The most complicated legal technicalities that a collector faces today lie in sound reproductions. A collector who decides to gather recordings of any kind—transcriptions made in the presence of speakers and singers or from broadcasts of radio and television or as copies of other recordings—must proceed with a kind of caution not always necessary in handling written texts.

For example, both lyrics and music of a great mass of popular song mix genuine folk material, impromptu original addition, and occasional conscious or unconscious plagiarism, not to mention varying musical arrangement. The kind of oral narrative sometimes called the "traveling anecdote" presents similar mixture. Travel of some such stories began with a single author's composition in a copyrighted book.

Thus, in collecting artifacts of imagination, knowledge, or human experience, the collector may face vague questions that arise when public good and private right do not conform to precise, or precisely the same, terms. No collector who understands his field and rudimentary legal restrictions need be daunted. If he is aware of real uncertainty, however, legal advice may be needed. Generally, the collector can be assured that the law is as ready to protect rights of owners of the physical manuscript as it is to protect the interests of author and publisher who have original and basic interest in literary property. But copyright lawyers are properly disinclined to give a client merely comforting assurance. Hence the following amateur suggestions.

— If possible, before finally acquiring a manuscript, the collector should determine whether it is published or unpublished. If the text is unpublished or substantially different from the published version, the collector usually acquires only personal property in the physical manuscript. Unless copyright is specifically acquired by his purchase or by later assignment, his uses of the manuscript are limited.

— Even a collector of manuscripts on a modest scale is almost sure to be approached, and sometimes importuned, to allow indiscriminate use of his collection. Before allowing reproduction, the collector would do well to ask for a simple statement holding him harmless if copyright should be invaded. Getting advice from a lawyer before beginning any general program of lending, reproducing, or publishing is simple prudence.

— Collectors might well keep up with changing law. A good, short comment on literary property rights is James Thorpe's *The Use of Manuscripts in Literary Research*, published in 1974 by the Modern Language Association. Professor Thorpe's discussion is directed primarily to scholarly work in manuscripts held by libraries, but his lucid summaries touch upon numerous points that affect the private collector.

— Finally, in the spirit of the 1710 statute and the sense of our own Constitution's protection of copyright and patent, it is wise for the collector to define both purpose and procedure in the encouragement of learning. Although the possibility of falling afoul of the law is remote, a pure heart and high purpose are little defense if the collector invades another's property rights. It is better to protect those rights beforehand than to argue about good intentions with an irate writer, an offended heir, or a thwarted publisher.

Fact and Artifact:
Memory and Understanding

Address, Association of American Archivists, U.T. Austin, 1964

ALTHOUGH I am not an archivist, I have some deep personal convictions on the subject of archives. This is neither a disclaimer nor an opening pleasantry, but a simple introduction to the opinions that follow.

First, I should like to say a word in appreciation of those preservers of the human record in the long generations before *archive* became a clearly defined term, before that term was given historical significance and scholarly vitality by professional archivists. Like much of our learned vocabulary (such as the closely allied word *library*) and despite the wisdom and skill of those who translate vocabulary into action, the public and popular conception of an "archive" is still somewhat shaky in its application and not a little ambiguous in popular and public uses. I have made no scientific count of these verbal deviations and proliferations; but within the period of my own intense interest in the preservation, good order, efficient management, and wise service of what I would call "archives" I have found this label used for

—a collection of oil well cores;

—ninety-one cartons of dust jackets;

—a disused collection of college entrance examinations;

—forty thousand circus posters;

—the love letters of a great poet who knew what he was doing, together with the composition books of a verse writer who didn't;

— a collection of pamphlets from the office of a local political club;

— a warehouse full of magician's paraphernalia and that magician's collection of beeswax sculpture;

— one thousand cases of punched cards on juvenile delinquency, unintelligible to the naked eye but presumably intelligible to one make of machine;

— ten times one thousand cases containing magnetized tape— with the same rate of increasing intelligibility;

— forty volumes of clipped signatures of George Washington, Thomas Jefferson, and others, including candidates for president.

In an age of so many artifacts and with so many diverse passions for recovering, preserving, and interpreting all sorts of visible evidence of man's past, one must pause—at least for breath. I suggest that the founders, directors, and users of archives should also take longer pauses for meditation, for rational discrimination, and for planning.

Without attempting to make a bowknot of my four-way topic— fact and artifact, memory and understanding—I have some points to suggest. Please take them gently, as coming from an interested outsider.

First, we need much greater skill in distinguishing the significant from the insignificant. There are points at which the papers of the very small may be more revealing than certain documents of the very great. It is hardly revealing that a president in 1908 regretted that he could not attend a venison dinner on Wednesday.

Second, we must be increasingly alert to the false and the genuine. If collectors, scholars, and archivists are not aware that there is an international forgery business now making millions of dollars annually, they are sure to be shaken awake rudely—and only a little less rudely if they are collectors of forgery.

Third, those of us whose main experience spans the transition from Spencerian hand to typewriter must hasten our adjustments to microfilm and microprint and get on to new electronic record.

We must get ready for all new forms of record: audible, visible, and symbolic.

Fourth, we must also learn new combinations of our resources and new ways to mass, focus, analyze, and interpret these resources.

Finally, we must stay alive to the public responsibility that curatorship of public and private record imposes. This curatorship once required only a sort of loving care and a reasonable amount of systematic attention. Today it involves knowledge, policy, and law. The problems are as varied as deterioration, copyright, the invasion of privacy, the techniques of duplication, and the means of discriminating among users: the expert, the knowledgeable, the curious, the idle, the irresponsible, and the destructive users.

More than historical record depends upon the archivist today and tomorrow. The understanding of history (in all its aspects) may, and in some quarters must, account for the understanding and wisdom by which future history is still to be made and recorded.

University Presses

Address, Association of American University Presses,
U.T. Austin, 1973

MY own debt to university presses goes back many years. I got my first real sense of printed things in the rooms of a tiny college press. In those days all its type was set by hand. The presiding man of fonts was Albert Chalmers Sneed. He is nowhere recorded, I suppose, in annals of printing; but he was what many of his successors at presses across the country have been—highly talented, overworked, underpaid, insufficiently budgeted, tireless in pursuit of accuracy and grace, contemptuous of pretense, and impatient about those academic habits which he defined as "muddying up good paper with forgettable words."

Complex deliberations that academic publishers undertake (as well as multiplying difficulties that the press must face) give me pause. I am reminded of a symbolic chart of research communications presented some years ago to a national committee. Those who would discuss it frankly could never decide whether it looked like an inverted copy of an old scriptural etching of the Tower of Babel or had been taken straight from the somewhat more awesome drawings of Dante's successive infernal circles. I remember that at the soaring and widening top there was a legend something like "multimedia input-output" and at the nethermost level something else called, with old, familiar starkness, "the word."

It is obvious that the current generation of directors of university presses have new and enlarging problems: finances, merchandising and other kinds of distribution, recruitment, space, equipment. The list is a long one.

The opposite side of this coin of perplexity is sometimes made to seem too shiny. New technologies, new devices, new kinds of readership, new combinations of materials or media can be overestimated. Yet we cannot afford to ignore long-range opportunity any more than we can brush aside instant crisis.

I assume that there are no easy formulas for university publishing in any context. Without resort to formularies, here are some general proposals.

— A great national depository where all university press books in print could be seen by institutional representatives and orders placed by what are now called "emerging libraries." Today an increasing number of new academic reference collections begin by first acquiring works issued by university presses. Yet the labor of selection from separate lists or even from joint listings of these presses is prodigious, and, to the buyer for the educational institution, expensive.

— A systematic, and therefore carefully controlled, program of publication at both the top and the bottom of book design. That program would include a few beautifully designed, meticulously manufactured volumes priced high and never remaindered. A much larger number of studies, utility books, or highly experimental (and therefore financially hazardous) publications would be produced as cheaply as possible. The shelves between would lodge the mass of university print.

— A register of manuscripts available for university press publication. Entry might assume that the manuscript had been submitted to at least one press and refused. Even if that assumption offended scholarly pride, it would at least reduce numerous useless submissions of a manuscript, often made at random, to presses that for various reasons would not possibly undertake its publication.

— A similar register, necessarily less specific, of positive interests of the presses and of those categories in which particular presses are not currently interested. This device would correct the assumption that all university publishing programs follow exactly the same pattern.

— Insistence on brevity. Among the relatively serious works that most university presses publish, many are two, three, or four times too long. Neither brevity nor lengthiness guarantees significance, of course.

— Encouragement of major national organizations of educational administrators to consider periodically the problems of academic publication. During many years of attending meetings of such organizations, I have heard this subject discussed on rare occasions. Like directors of presses, university administrators almost always discuss immediate problems. The case for the press therefore must be made periodically.

— Special discounts to graduate students. Most oncoming scholars wait for that indefinite time when books they want upon publication may be remaindered. Sometimes they must await a still later year when they can afford essential books then outdated or out of print.

— Apprenticeship. Younger academics should be made aware of the numerous careers to which the university press can introduce them. Presses should be enabled, at low stipend, to offer them apprenticeship.

— Endowment. Not many schoolmen can say with more conviction than I feel that every faculty needs more permanent endowment for teaching and research positions. I think that equally sensible is the endowment of university presses to support publication of current scholarly, highly experimental, or creative work. Many of us have argued that publication of research is a kind of teaching. It is also subject to criticism more rigorous than that of seminar or classroom performance. Of course, a great deal of research writing must be judged as not worthy of publication or capable of being made instructive by revision. In any case, I would argue for publication endowment if only because such endowment imposes upon management of practical affairs a continuing trusteeship in the moral and intellectual sense.

Beset by many other kinds of responsibility, a university press cannot be expected to act as a formal teaching department. It can be an effective agency, however, for providing practical information about the physical nature of the artifacts of information, book to microfiche.

Two generations ago it was considered almost irrelevant, if not slightly beneath the dignity of the philological student, to know how books are made and circulated. In those days, scholars enjoyed a profession of innocence about almost everything practical. The scholar knew little about his role under laws of literary property, although he recognized plagiarism in freshman themes as a manifest problem. The implications of printing in multiple faces (including letters of obscure language), reproduction in color, the practicalities of proofreading were among the subjects considered foreign to the intellectual who also wrote. Thanks in part to descriptive and analytical bibliography, this widespread handicap to publication has been partly corrected. There is still need of the kind of practical guidance a press can give the burgeoning scholar and his elders who have not taken the trouble to learn anything about manufacturing the wares of intellect.

One can hope that, when the history of university publishing in the United States is written, fugitive pieces printed and issued in college and university towns will not be totally neglected. There have been numerous examples of what I mean. To cite one: the first translation of Lobachevski's non-Euclidean geometry (by way of Gauss' German text) was privately printed in Austin decades ago by a mathematician named George Bruce Halsted.

To sum up, there has never been a time when the essential activity of university presses has had greater need of immediate, steadfast support. The expense of communicating rapidly increasing discovery and creation cannot be subsidized by ambition, tradition, or sentiment. It requires financial support.

Intellectual standards of a university can be judged in many contexts and on many bases. Year in and year out, no context is more reliable than a university's publications. The university press is more than important; it is essential to the fulfillment of a university's highest obligations.

Development of Research Collections at The University of Texas

Address, American Library Association, Austin, 1971*

I HAVE been asked to discuss informally some phases of growth in the Humanities Research Center collections in relatively recent years—approximately the decades of the fifties and sixties. I will speak to facts and not attempt to prophesy.

Among necessary exclusions I find it difficult to omit the history of elder libraries on this campus: Palm and Garcia, Wrenn and Aitken, Stark and DeGolyer, extensive holdings of the Texas and Latin American collections, as well as numerous college, school, and departmental divisions.

Many of the separate resources sometimes identified in professional surveys as "TxU" have new and encouraging opportunities for the future. Central to these prospects is the University General Library, itself, expansion of which has been recommended steadily during the years I have known Texas. As to the larger book map of the state, I find it still harder to be silent about the distinction of institutional and private collections located in this region but not affiliated with The University of Texas System.

As to retrospect, initial plans for new development of research collections at Austin were first suggested in 1952. I have been asked repeatedly to state the purpose of those plans. Explanation of that purpose has not changed since then: it is simply "to make

---

* Delivered to the Rare Books Section of the Association of College and Research Libraries of the American Library Association.

Published in another version by *Bookman's Weekly*, 1971.

a good library better." That was the key phrase in my 1952 proposal. If it seems fuzzy, I can re-word it. Some day The University of Texas should have a very good library.

Both this suggestion and formal proposals to the Regents in 1957 were based on practical considerations. Since 1897 the University had acquired more than one research collection on which to build. Austin was farther from each coast, and from almost anywhere else, than it is today. Both graduate programs and undergraduate studies were moving in new directions and at fast pace. Given these conditions, collecting entire libraries for research was one means of improvement.

A practical reason for beginning with emphasis on writing in the United States and England during a recent period (approximately 1850 to 1950) was that relevant collections were available. They were not so widely sought and used, nor were they so highly priced, as they are today. Chronological and geographical limits of the initial plan did not last long. As the sixties disappeared, the 1950 date was moved forward and 1850 was moved back. Unexpected opportunity encouraged wider scope. U.S.-English boundaries were therefore expanded to include Ireland, Scotland, Australia, France, Italy, Germany, and other countries. Geographical and chronological limits are still moving outward. Influence upon twentieth-century thinking and living cannot be limited by date or by regions of the globe in which that influence originates. That is a fancy way of saying, "Get what you need when you can if the library can afford it or a donor will give it."

Some of the more difficult early decisions had to do with peripheries of what great philologians had taught my generation to call "literature," convinced that we knew what we meant by that word. The history of design and architecture, maps and charts, the Western novel, detective fiction, and the little magazine (often short-lived, sometimes vital while it lasted) are mixed examples that escape but do not dishonor older tradition.

The term "humanities" was stretched to include broad relationships rather than academic compartments, so that the natural sciences and their history as well as some topics in the social sciences and their practice were included later. So were graphic arts in general, printing in particular, and the history of religions not confined to doctrine.

At this point I would put a series of random observations. Some of them are recorded fact; others are mere personal opinion and therefore arguable.

— It is a fact that there could have been no such program without the steady support and approval of both the Board of Regents and other agencies of the state.

— An overworked staff, patient members of the faculty, and constructive critics inside and outside the University have made regular progress possible.

— There could have been some sort of development, but it would have been much less significant without the generous help of donors, about half of whom have been neither citizens of Texas nor former students of the University. They have tripled the program's activity.

— Every collecting library, like all independent collectors, must stay indebted, as Texas does, to the book business, especially to the perceptive bookseller.

— Arithmetic of the book world requires interpretation. For example, we can say that approximately two hundred collections— ranging from 100,000 items to less than a dozen—have been joined together in what some of us like to consider the intellectual vintage of the years since Texas became a state. But counting printed titles, leaves of manuscript, photographs and maps, and other artifacts for inventory is less significant than use of the materials. Hence I would emphasize the number of mature scholars and younger students who were assisted rather than statistics about mass holdings. There is no reliable means of quick and quantitative measurement of research; evaluation may differ from scholar to scholar and from time to time. Similarly, "book prices current" are useful records, but "values permanent," even though they may require ten or fifty years to describe, are closer to our purposes.

— As to muddled, misleading, and sometimes prejudiced or deliberately false report, I doubt that research libraries suffer more than kindred programs devoted to the preservation of records and the exchange of ideas. They suffer less now than do the newly essential computation sciences from exaggeration, jest, and misunderstanding.

— As to mistakes, every research library makes them. Both errant decision and triumphant success should be reexamined at intervals. One of the livelier ironies of the book world is that what may seem to have been sheer biblidiocy in the immediate event can turn out to be a stroke of unexpected blessing at some later date. Conversely, with the passage of time, triumphs can turn out to be merely routine or empty accomplishment. About the research library generally, therefore, I would suggest that, whether or not we can give it instant credence, we should at least give it time.

I will conclude with a different kind of list: operational problems of research collections.

— First is the problem of accessibility. Large acquisition always makes access to printed works difficult. The backlog of uncatalogued pieces in most of the great libraries of the world is evidence of this fact. As to manuscripts (except for a few small collections accepted under seal for a period of time), resources of the research center have been made almost instantly available. A university, however, cannot give access to manuscripts that it has not acquired and does not expect to acquire, despite widespread reports that it has them safely stowed. Nor can it handle large masses of material until a reasonably systematic record is completed. Even then, some scholarly expectations must be disappointed. Research librarians are acquainted with such urgent requests as "Please send copies of all the material you have now or acquire later on writer X or topic Y. I am writing a book."

— Writing for publication—even writing a dissertation—should be undertaken with at least rudimentary knowledge of laws on copyright and invasion of privacy. A scholar may choose to break these laws at his own peril, but he has no constitutional right to imperil the library, the librarian, or his publisher. For practical purposes, it has been true since the publication of Pope's letters that copyright in manuscript lasts as long as the author lasts, and longer—in most instances for an additional fifty years after the death of the author. As to privacy, restriction is not merely polite consideration for those involved. It is also encouragement to preserve records that otherwise will likely be destroyed by sensitive and overcautious heirs.

— Priority of use is closely related to both the preceding problems. In general terms, competence of the applicant and a chronological order of requests, kept active for a reasonable period (three years, five years, seven years) will serve. Like Texas, most universities rely upon a committee of the faculty to determine practice.

— Avoidance of competition in developing libraries is possible when clear understanding can be reached beforehand. Texas has deferred repeatedly to institutional and other public libraries as well as to private collectors when it was possible to do so.

If one believes, as I do, that it is nonsense to assume that the market is now barren of collectible print and that there are no new fields for collection, this decade's main problems will be finances and new laws affecting collection. No research library can do everything; none should attempt even all that it might choose to do. Unless I have received false reports, financial limitations will soon appear in many library programs. To such obvious limitations must now be added restrictions upon gifts of "self-created" collections. And plain talk by tax attorneys and tax accountants makes it clear that we will soon confront new perplexities governing gifts from foundations, especially those that are private.

What encourages me in the midst of these confusions is the sustained and vigorous generosity of the friends of libraries. I do not mean dues-paying organizations alone. The great potential still lies in common interest motivated by common sense in the cause of common cultural heritage. Given that asset, I refuse to greet the future with that lack of cheer which is the occupational ailment of all of us concerned with budgets.

I began by saying that I would not attempt prophecy here. The disclaimer did not deny me a right to hope. I hope

— that the rewards of discovery will always exceed prices at auction;

— that the broadest possible encouragement of inquiry and study will offset both pride of shelves and stupid sense of property;

— that, finally, peace and unity will continue their habitation in libraries—apparently one of the few social contexts left capable of making both unity and peace feel completely at home.